Secrets to Contacting

CELEBRITIES & PUBLIC FIGURES

101 Ways to Reach the Rich & Famous

JORDAN MCAULEY

Mega Niche Media

Activate Your Free
30-Day Membership To:

Contact Any Celebrity
www.ContactAnyCelebrity.com

Your #1 Source for Accurate Celebrity Contact Information ($30.00 Value!)

To register your Celebrity Black Book 2008 and START YOUR FREE 30-DAY ONLINE MEMBERSHIP, visit:

www.contactanycelebrity.com/free

You'll get Instant Access to the Best Mailing Address, Agent, Manager, Publicist, Production Company and Charitable Cause for Over 55,565 Celebrities and Public Figures Worldwide!

It's that easy!

You'll get Instant Access
to all this and more:

Easy-To-Use Searchable Database

The Best Mailing Addresses For

Over 55,565 Celebrities Worldwide

Agent, Manager & Publicist Info

Celebrity Charitable Causes

Daily Real-Time Updates

Free Research Requests

Postage Refund Guarantee

Professional Tips & Advice

Toll-Free 24/7 Customer Service

Celebrity Gift Bag Opportunities

Plus much more!

Activate Your Free 30-Day Online Membership:

www.contactanycelebrity.com/free

Also by Jordan McAuley

Books

The Celebrity Black Book
www.CelebrityBlackBook.com

Celebrity Leverage
www.CelebrityLeverage.com

Help from Hollywood
www.HelpFromHollywood.com

Databases

Celebrity Causes Database
www.CelebCauses.com

Contact Any Celebrity
www.ContactAnyCelebrity.com

Resources

Celebrity Book Endorsements Toolkit
www.BookEndorsements.com

Celebrity Endorsements System
www.CelebrityEndorsements.com

How to Hire a Celebrity
www.HowToHireACelebrity.com

Make Your Book Famous
www.MakeYourBookFamous.com

Secrets to Contacting

CELEBRITIES
&PUBLIC
FIGURES

101 Ways to Reach the Rich & Famous

"Indispensable."
–Autograph Magazine

JORDAN MCAULEY

Secrets to Contacting Celebrities and Public Figures:
101 Ways to Reach the Rich and Famous.

Mega Niche Media
8721 Santa Monica Blvd., #431
West Hollywood, CA 90069-4507
310–388–6084 (Phone)
310–388–6084 (Fax)
www.MegaNiche.com

Visit Contact Any Celebrity at **www.ContactAnyCelebrity.com** to search our online database of over 54,000 celebrities and public figures worldwide for the best mailing address, agent, manager, and publicist.

Cover Design and Interior Design: Desktop Miracles, Inc.

ATTENTION: Quantity discounts are available on bulk purchases of this book for reselling, educational purposes, subscription incentives, gifts or fundraising. Special books or book excerpts can also be created to fit specific needs. For more information, contact our Special Sales Department at Mega Niche Media, 8721 Santa Monica Blvd., #431, West Hollywood, CA 90069–4507.

Although the author and publisher have made every effort to ensure the accuracy and completeness of the information contained in this book, we assume no responsibility for errors, inaccuracies, omissions, or any inconsistency herein. Any slight of people, places or organizations is unintentional.

Manufactured in the United States of America
Library of Congress Control Number: 2008924664
ISBN–10: 1–60487–001-X
ISBN–13: 978–1–60487–001–5

This book is dedicated to all Members,
past and present, of Contact Any Celebrity
(www.ContactAnyCelebrity.com).

Your patronage, loyalty, feedback and friendships
mean more than you will ever know.

Table of Contents

*"I'll worry when they stop asking
me for my autograph."*

—KATHARINE HEPBURN

Introduction

*"You know, Mama, one day some other
young girl is going to make her way across
this room and ask for my autograph."*

—JAYNE MANSFIELD

So You Want to Contact a Celebrity . . .

I'm assuming that since you're reading this book, you want to make contact with one or more celebrities. This book will show you how to do it. Filled with insider tips, tricks, and techniques, *Secrets to Contacting Celebrities & Public Figures* will show you everything you need to know to reach the stars— literally!

Maybe you want an autograph from your favorite actor. Or perhaps you'd like your photo taken with your favorite singer. Or maybe you're looking to get your favorite baseball player to sign a jersey for your little brother who is sick. Whatever your need for contacting a celebrity, this book will help you succeed. In fact, if you totaled my tips up, you'd find more than 101 ways in this book to achieve contact with well-known and sought-after individuals.

Of course, this information is not about stalking. I do not condone invading a celebrity's personal life or trespassing on private property. Instead, this book is about how to contact your favorite star or celebrity at events, concerts, live appearances, book-signings, conventions and even through the mail.

As the Founder of **Contact Any Celebrity** (www.ContactAnyCelebrity.com) and the editor of the best-selling *Celebrity Black Book* (www.CelebrityBlackBook.com), I've spoken with collectors, fan club presidents, agents, managers, publicists, journalists, photographers, assistants and even the stars themselves about how to do this the right way. Some of the methods contained in this book are more questionable than others, but they are all legal. Morals are subjective, and the choices are for you to make on your own.

How to Use This Book

In the past, contacting or meeting celebrities may have seemed difficult or even impossible to you. Soon you'll see that it's actually very possible. This book delivers the "how to" you need to succeed, and I've organized it in the following way to make your options as clear and doable as possible.

Part I, "Insider Secrets—All the Right Moves," starts with this introductory chapter. It then continues with three additional chapters which will help you develop basic skills so you'll be able to move forward with your plans successfully.

Chapter 1   "Getting Autographs"
Chapter 2   "Doing Your Research"
Chapter 3   "Contacting Celebrities on MySpace"

Part II, "Tips for Contacting Certain Types of Celebrities," then gives you the lowdown on the specifics for approaching the kinds of stars that interest you. A separate chapter is devoted to each category of celebrity. Once you have your basic skills developed from reading Part I, you can jump ahead to the chapters in Part II that are relevant to you.

Part II starts with "Actors & Actresses," and progresses to "Musicians," then "Talk Show Hosts" and "Program Hosts & News Anchors." This is followed by seven chapters for different types of sports figures, from "Baseball Players" to "Wrestlers." After that, there's a short chapter on "Politicians & Heads of State." Next you'll find "Authors" and "Comic Book Artists and Writers."

Finally, Part II concludes with three chapters on some of today's sexiest celebrities, "Supermodels," "Playboy Playmates," and "Adult Film Stars &

Centerfold Models." You'll also find helpful supplementary information in the back of the book, including Resources, a Bonus Article by an actual TV Producer, and a list of Common Autograph Terms that insiders use.

Send Me Your Success Stories!

By the way, I'd love to hear your success stories related to using this book. Feel free to email them to me at jordan@contactanycelebrity.com.

You can also send your success stories to me here:

Jordan McAuley
Contact Any Celebrity
8721 Santa Monica Blvd., #431
W. Hollywood, CA 90069-4507
Or fax them to: 310-362-8771

Ready? Let's Go!

Now you know the basics. What you need to do at this point is to keep reading and get your camera loaded. I'm about to give you all the info you'll ever need to get in touch with your favorite celebrities, and have the stars actually be happy you did!

But before we dive into the material, here's a valuable tip. If you get on my private email list, I'll send you free Celebrity Addresses of the Week—plus updated tricks and techniques on contacting celebrities which are not included in this book.

To sign up, visit Contact Any Celebrity at www.ContactAnyCelebrity.com.

While you're there, you can also search my exclusive online database for over 54,000 celebrities and public figures containing such contact information as the best mailing address, agent, manager, publicist, production company and/or charitable cause.

OK, let's get going! We'll start by looking at collecting autographs . . .

Part One

. . . .

Insider Secrets—
All the Right Moves

chapter
ONE

Getting Great Autographs

"Always give an autograph when somebody asks you."

—TOMMY LASORDA

Autographs used to be a way of proving you had really met a famous person—the way a signature in a hotel guest book could prove that Abraham Lincoln had actually slept there. Today, however, most autographs that are collected either disappear in a drawer, in the trash, or they end up in collectible stores and in online auctions like eBay.

"I remember whenever I got good grades in school, my mom would say, 'Congratulations, do you want to go to What's on Second?' [a local sports collectibles store]," says New England Patriots' Superbowl-winning quarterback Tom Brady. "I'd always say, 'Let's go!' The card market is pretty amazing. When you have something signed by someone you admired as a kid, you feel like you have a little piece of them. It's just continued to grow, mainly because people seem to have a fixation; they like to buy baseball cards. We're asked to participate in a lot of card shows, and it isn't until you get there that you realize how big a deal the card industry really is. Shoot, the whole memorabilia industry is amazing now. To think that Luis Gonzalez's gum went for as much as it did; that's amazing to me."

By the way, Luis Gonzalez's gum really did go for a large amount of money on eBay—$10,000 in fact—leading Seattle Mariner's relief pitcher Jeff Nelson to try and sell bone chips from his elbow on the service soon after. Unfortunately for him, eBay has a rule against selling body parts, so Nelson's auction was soon cancelled.

Be aware that an autograph can just as easily be junk as it can be treasure. Tom Brady knows this from experience, having had to tell more than one memorabilia store owner that a football in their possession supposedly signed by him was really a forgery. "When you talk about how big of a business autographs is, and how much money is involved, you can understand why people are trying to cut corners. I know I'm a little apprehensive when I see older guys standing outside waiting for my autograph."

The only way to be sure that the autograph is genuine, whether it comes from an athlete, actor, musician, or serial killer (yes, people collect autographs from them as well), is to make contact with the person yourself (well, maybe not the serial killer). This can be difficult with some celebrities, but others are very easy to track down and are more than willing to offer you their signature for your collection. If you're smart, sane, and prepared to do a little home (and leg) work, you can contact just about any celebrity out there and let them know how much you appreciate their work.

Of course, getting an autograph on a piece of memorabilia like a baseball, a script, or a movie poster—as opposed to a blank piece of paper—is best because it adds value. It also makes the autograph suitable for framing or for display in your home or office.

In-Person vs. Mailed or Sold

Not everyone seeking an autograph is a real fan. Many people are professionally employed autograph seekers, and some spend hours every day in pursuit of a celebrity moniker, earning up to six figures a year in the process.

An "in-person" autograph seeker heads to places where celebrities are known to hang out—a store or a hot restaurant—and they'll wait . . . and wait . . . and wait. When they finally do spot a celebrity, the most hardcore autograph hunters will go to their car and delve through some of the thousands of headshots they keep on hand—just in case—to find the right ones. These autograph seekers usually ask for more than one photo to be signed so they can sell them to autograph dealers. However celebrities don't like this, and it may be the reason they refuse to give you an autograph.

Other times, the professionals will work in concert with people in other businesses like limo drivers, bell boys, or maitre d's who will call and let them know when someone famous is inside. But not every celebrity is willing to sign, especially when they know they're dealing with a professional who's going to make a lot of money off their name. Stars like Tobey Maguire, Cameron Diaz, and Britney Spears have been notoriously unlikely to put a pen to picture, and actors like Sean Penn and Edward Norton can make a scene when they say no.

"I can always tell a genuine fan and an eBay junkie," Ewan McGregor reportedly told London's Daily Star, adding that he might not bother signing any more autographs in the future since so many show up on eBay. Some stars like Madonna and Julia Roberts only sign autographs for charity. Yet others like George Clooney and Angelina Jolie seem to be more than happy to sign a photo when asked.

In Person

Spotting a celebrity at the mall or on the street can be an exciting experience. Just remember, they're people, too. They're not wild animals that have just escaped from the zoo, although I'm sure they feel that way at times. Here are some basic points to remember when you do spot your favorite celebrity out and about:

Stay calm. You don't want to frighten your celebrity away!

Smile. People usually respond positively to smiling since this makes them feel more comfortable (unless the smile is coming from Jack Nicholson in *Batman*!).

Be informed. Know who it is you just spotted. If all you have in mind to say is: "Aren't you the guy who played that guy . . . ," then you should probably not approach the celebrity.

Don't interrupt. If the celebrity is on the phone, eating, in the bathroom, or talking to someone else, just leave them alone. If they happen to be with their children, don't bother them—and in particular don't hassle their kids.

Keep moving. Don't hang around and freak them out. Step back and talk to someone else until you see that there's a lull in the conversation or they're about to leave.

Be real. As J-Lo likes to point out, she's still "Jenny from the Block." Whether you believe that statement or not, treat each celebrity with some common courtesy, and try to talk to them like they're real people.

Stay low-key. If you talk loudly or cause a big scene, the celebrity will most likely be out of there faster than Jennifer and Ben's *Gigli* was out of the theatres.

Be creative. "Would you mind signing this for my kid?" usually seems to work—even if you don't have a kid. (You didn't hear that from me!)

In contrast to showing courtesy to celebrities, during the past few decades there have been incidents of star stalking turned ugly. A woman obsessed with Brad Pitt pushed herself through an open window to enter his house, slept in his bed, wore his clothes, and was found with a book of witchcraft and a long needle with ribbons around one end. (We don't want to know what that was for!) Pitt was then granted a restraining order against the teenager.

A Madonna fan chose the wrong superstar to mess with when he climbed over the wall to her house after reportedly asking her to marry him and threatening her repeatedly, and he was shot several times by her security guard. Madonna's stalker ultimately was sentenced to 10 years in prison for his actions. Most recently, an Uma Thurman fan who sent letters to the star threatening to kill himself if he saw her with another man was indicted on stalking charges. Of course, he didn't just send a letter. The man also tried to get into her trailer by claiming he was a friend when she was filming a movie in New York.

However, you don't have to be a complete psycho to be accused of stalking. Many people have been accused of invading a celebrity's personal space for being just a little too persistent. See the sidebar "The Good, The Bad, and the Ugly" below for insight on how to stay in safe territory.

The Good, the Bad and the Ugly . . . or How Not to Be a Stalker

The tips below will help make sure you don't meet your favorite celebrity . . . in court.

Example 1—Stop the Paparazzi!

Good: Spotting a celebrity on the street and asking if they'd mind having their photo taken with you.

Bad: Taking the celebrity's photo without permission as he or she eats dinner at a restaurant.

Ugly: Taking the celebrity's photo without their permission as they head into their plastic surgeon's or therapist's office.

Example 2—Fan Mail

Good: Sending a letter to a celebrity telling them about your favorite movies that they've been in.

Bad: Sending 18 letters to a celebrity telling them about your favorite movies that they've been in.

Ugly: Sending 18 letters to a celebrity telling them about the voices in your head that tell you to kill.

Example 3—Celebrity Book-Signing

Good: Showing up at a book-signing and purchasing the book that the celebrity recently wrote, then asking them to sign it.

Bad: Showing up at a book-signing with an unauthorized biography about the celebrity that he or she didn't write and asking them to sign it.

Ugly: Spitting on the celebrity at their book-signing because you disagree with his or her past actions. (This actually happened to Jane Fonda at a recent book-signing for her autobiography, *My Life So Far*!).

By Mail

Since the odds of spontaneously running into your favorite star on the street are somewhat low, I'll address the best ways to reach him or her by mail.

Most celebrities receive fan mail every day. Some get thousands of letters each week, which is why their mail is sometimes handled by other people employed by the stars. These people come in the form of personal assistants, managers, publicists, and agents. When mail is received, the person opening it usually sorts it into three piles. These stacks divide the mail into things to be discarded, requests for autographed photos, and "special" correspondence. Falling into that last category are letters from people who claim to know the celebrity or letters that tell a good story which might interest the star. Sometimes it includes letters from people who have simply put in a lot of effort. This last coveted pile is where you want to your letter to be placed.

So How Do You Make Sure Your Correspondence Gets Noticed?

Well, there's a fine line between making a letter personal and meaningful to a celebrity and sending something that freaks them out and puts you on their list of potential stalkers. (Yes, these lists really do exist.) See the sidebar below to get a sense of how to be seen favorably.

Meaningful or Creepy?

Not sure of the difference when it comes to how you write your letters to celebrities? Here are some clarifying examples.

Example 1—Kinship

Meaningful: Discussing how you're a friend of the celebrity's uncle.

Creepy: Telling the celebrity that you slept with his or her uncle.

Example 2—A Reel Fan

Meaningful: Stating how you've always respected the person's work.

Creepy: Telling them you have 18 copies of their first film.

Example 3—Photo Opp

Meaningful: Including a nice photo of you waving hello.

Creepy: Including a nude shot of yourself.

Including your photo is a good way to get noticed enough to have something personal sent back. When the celebrity or celebrity's assistant can put a face with your letter, it's less likely they'll treat it like the 1,600 others in front of them. Remember Rosie O'Donnell's talk show where she'd always talk about a letter she received from a "cutie patootie"? That's what I mean. Or watch Ellen DeGeneres's talk show and notice how she mentions things people have sent her that almost always include a photo she can show on TV.

Professional autograph hounds usually include an unsigned 8x10 photo of the celebrity, plus a Sharpie pen and a self-addressed stamped envelope to make it as easy as possible for the star to sign the photo and send it back. Doing this, however, sometimes makes the celebrity or assistant think the signed photo will only end up on eBay, which they don't like.

Instead, be personal. Reveal how the celebrity's personality or work has had an impact on you. Did they get you to exercise more? To explore a different culture? To treat your kids better? The easiest rule of thumb is to think "if I received a letter like this out of hundred of others and didn't know the person, would I take it to heart?"

Follow the rules below and you'll find yourself getting signed photos back in the mail in no time:

Be polite. Whether you're requesting an autograph in person or through the mail, remember that celebrities may be famous but they don't owe you anything.

Be original. If you use a form letter, it will be obvious from the start that you don't really care about them.

Be personable. Tell the person what you admire about them, but don't fawn.

Concentrate on things the celebrity has achieved that make them proud instead of parts in films that brought them money but little satisfaction. For instance, if you're writing Angelina Jolie, talk about how much you admire the fact that she donates so much time, energy and money to humanitarian issues around the world and has adopted three children. That will most likely get a better response than "I loved you in *Tomb Raider*."

Be positive. Don't touch on negative things in the person's life, and try to steer clear of your own problems unless the story you're telling depends on it. If you lost your leg in a mosh pit at a Marilyn Manson concert, then by all means go into great detail (he'd probably like that). But trust me . . . Martha Stewart does not want to hear about your enlarged prostate or the lover who dumped you. And Martha especially doesn't want to be reminded that she went to prison or is a convicted felon.

KISS. No, not the envelope. KISS is short for "Keep It Simple, Stupid!" No celebrity wants to read five pages of handwritten scrawl about your dog Muffin. Well, maybe Ellen does, but she's the exception.

Make it clear. Use a word-processing program like Microsoft Word to type and format your letter, and then print it out. Celebrities are busy—they do not have time to decipher your handwriting.

Make it easy. Include a folded 9x12 manila envelope with postage affixed (this is called a self-addressed stamped envelope or SASE) inside a larger 10x13 envelope. If you're not sure how much postage to include, ask your local post office or use an online service like Stamps.com to calculate and print exact postage from your computer. Celebrities may have a lot of money, but they're not going to pay for postage to reply to every fan letter they receive.

Include a photo. Also include your own photo of the celebrity. There are many places where you can buy them online. A great site to use to get quality unsigned celebrity photos is **Amazing Celebrity Photos** (www.AmazingCelebrityPhotos.com).

Most stars have headshots and still photos from their most recent film that they can sign and send you, however sometimes they run out. Including one of your own will make getting a reply that much easier.

Keep it short. Your letter should be only one to two pages typed, double-spaced.

Give a good reason. If you want the celebrity to write you back, you have to give them a reason. Asking a question is a great way to do this, especially if it relates to something the person loves.

When I was younger, I wrote a letter to Kathy Bates asking her what the word "Towanda" meant that she kept yelling in the movie *Fried Green Tomatoes*. She wrote me back on pig stationery (a nod to her role in *Misery*) that the word was a battle cry for an African Queen named Towanda, and that the scene where this was explained had been cut from the final version of the movie. (It's now included on the Collector's Edition DVD.) She later sent me a full-size *Fried Green Tomatoes* poster. At the time, Kathy Bates had just won an Oscar for *Misery*. So don't think that just because a celebrity is famous, they won't write back.

Ask for what you want. If you don't ask for a signed photo, you probably won't get one.

Be complete. Make sure everything you send has your name and address on it; sometimes material gets separated after the mail is opened. Put your details on the envelope, on the letter, on the back of the photo, on the SASE, etc. Put it on everything—just in case.

Be cheap. Don't send anything valuable that can't be replaced. There's no guarantee you'll get anything back. Maybe you'd really like Ben Affleck to sign that *Good Will Hunting* poster you bought. However, when that huge package gets delivered to his agent's office, it becomes more of a problem than a favor—especially with increased security regarding packages from unknown people. (This is true even if you send something via UPS or FedEx.) If you want Hilary Duff to sign a CD, just send the liner notes, not the entire disc. Remember, it's your problem if an item cost you a lot of money and it gets lost because you sent it to a celebrity.

Be reasonable. One per customer—do not send 15 items to be signed. This is supposed to be about a fan connecting with their favorite star and that star doing them a small favor, not making a fortune on eBay. Though you won't get in trouble for selling an autograph to make money (like an old one you no longer want), being respectful and courteous is always the best way to get a reply.

Be professional. Spell check, spell check, spell check! Making sure your grammar is correct couldn't hurt, either.

Be patient. Getting a reply normally takes six to eight weeks—sometimes sooner, sometimes later. If the celebrity is filming a movie on location and away from home, it can take a while. Some celebrities take up to a year to send back a reply. The key here is to be patient. Remember, good things come to those who wait!

Selling Your Autographs

If you do want to sell your autographs later on, there are many dealers you can try to sell them to. The best place to locate current autograph dealers is in *Autograph Magazine* (www.AutographMagazine.com), which you can usually find at large bookstores like Borders and Barnes & Noble. Each issue contains full-page ads for dealers listing what autographs they currently have for sale and how to contact them if you want to sell your collection. This is also a great magazine to subscribe to for news and updates on the world of autograph collecting. You can also sell or auction off your autographs online via eBay.

Join the Club!

You should also join the **UACC** (Universal Autograph Collectors Club) (www.UACC.org). This organization is the largest autograph club in the world, consisting of over 2,000 members in over 25 countries. They publish a 64-

page bimonthly journal called the Pen and Quill where members can buy, sell, and exchange autographs, and the UACC also holds seminars to educate collectors and the public on collecting and preserving autographs as well as identifying forgeries.

Is It Real?

As I mentioned earlier, the only way to know for sure that your autograph is real is to watch the celebrity sign it in person. However, you can also have it authenticated using one of the following services:

Collectors Universe (www.Collectors.com)

This is the leading provider of value-added grading and authentication services of high-end collectibles.

Is It Real (www.IsItReal.com)

This is an autograph opinion and reference service based in Germany. They provide free information on topics like what to look out for when buying autographs, and for-pay opinions of your autograph including "likely genuine" or "likely not genuine."

chapter TWO

Doing Your Research

*"Fame lost its appeal for me when I went into a
public restroom and an autograph seeker handed
me a pen and paper under the stall door."*

—MARLO THOMAS

Locating celebrities requires a little research. Here are
the best ways to find out if a celebrity will be in your area filming a movie,
making a live appearance, or showing up for a signing.

Search Engines

Searching for info about your favorite celebrity on an Internet search engine,
like **Google** (www.Google.com) or **Yahoo** (www.Yahoo.com), is a great way to start.
Often you can find out where and when the celebrity is scheduled to make an
appearance near you.

A few years ago, Yahoo was the #1 place to visit for online information.
However, over the last few years, it's turned into more of a brand and directory than an actual search engine. At the time of this writing, Google had

indexed more than four billion Web pages, more than 800 million images, and more than 845 million newsgroup messages. More than 81.9 million users visit Google every month, and 35 different languages are utilized. Why is it so popular? Because Google usually can provide the answers you seek.

Try these search phrases for starters. As you become more familiar with the search engine and how it works, you can make subtle changes to these example phrases. Don't worry, it really is easy! To begin, go to www.Google.com now and type in one of the following phrases, replacing [celebrity name] with someone you want information on:

[celebrity name] book signing
[celebrity name] charity event
[celebrity name] contact information
[celebrity name] email address

Refining Your Google Search

Here's an example of how to refine a search. If you try it online as you're reading, you'll find that the results have changed slightly since the time this particular search was done. That's because Google is constantly playing around with the search results they display. But the example below will give you a feeling for how to get the precise information that you're looking for.

Try typing in the words: Julianne Moore contact details. This will give you many results to look through, but knowing how to use Google means really knowing how to use Google! Many users don't realize that searching for that phrase will bring up pages with those words (Julianne and Moore and contact and details) displayed anywhere on its page.

That means you could get a page that was written by **Julianne** Smith about Roger **Moore**, where she says he can be contacted for a transcript of an interview the actor did with *Details* magazine.

In order to have Google truly narrow this search down to relevant results, we would need to add quotation marks. When we put quotes around two words (like "Julianne Moore"), Google will look for instances where those two words, names, or phrases will be shown together rather than just the pages where both appear anywhere. That is when we break out the plus sign (+).

Try a Google search for "Julianne Moore" + "contact details"—and now Google will return only Web sites where those two double-word phrases both occur. The difference is vast. In my original search with no quotation marks, Google turned up over 1,540,000 matches. But when I added quotation marks and the plus sign, it returned 910. We may still get bad results, however, even with such qualifiers. For example, if Julianne Moore, a student at XYZ Business School, is offering to tutor high school students and has put up a Web site with her contact details, that's going to show up in the search above.

Savvy searchers will add a little something extra to narrow down the searches even more. When I added the word "actress" to the mix, the results came down to 535]. Then I threw in "signed photo," and the results were reduced to just 104—a Web page that listed a postal address of Julianne Moore's agent. That was a good start, but I knew I could do even better.

The phrase "contact Julianne Moore" is a decent option. However, when I put that in Google, it returned a mere 102 results. Looking down the list, I saw that most of the results gave the same information: *the agent's address.* Some results didn't have any address at all, but instead have those words at the bottom of the page so they'd show up on Google searches . . . sneaky! Others were just portal Web sites, pointing to other Web sites with the actual information.

What I really wanted was an actual address that I'd feel confident using, so I decided that something else needed to be added to the search string. I chose a term I might find only in an actual address (example: "USA"). So I used "USA" when I conducted my new search, for a search of: "contact Julianne Moore" + "USA"—and I got 21 results, some of which listed an actual address. In this particular case, all of them were the agent's address, which is fine. At least I knew the information was probably factual and current.

But would a letter to that address result in a signed photo? And if did, would it be real or just a pre-printed signature? Another one of my Google searches answered that question pretty well: "Julianne Moore" + "signed photo" brought up a few Web pages where signed photos are sold, but it also brought up a Web site where an autograph collector had listed his successes in sending away for signed photos—and one of those was from Julianne Moore. When I clicked on the picture, I could see that it was signed "Dear Daniel," which would indicate that Ms. Moore signs her own photos. Bingo!

Also, something else worth noting is that while I was doing a later search on the Internet, I found a Web site which lists a contact address used with *c/o Laws of Attraction*, a movie that Moore was making in 2003. This is an insider tip— sending correspondence to the production company of whatever movie a star is currently filming is much less likely to result in a pre-printed signature, because not many people are writing them there! (To find the addresses of production companies, check industry trade magazines like *Variety* (www.Variety.com) and *The Hollywood Reporter* (www.HollywoodReporter.com). You'll learn more about these publications later in this chapter.).

So you can see that I just spent a little time narrowing down the right mailing address, and got info showing that Moore will likely give us a real autograph, and that she's open to fan contact—not to mention working out the best way to get in touch with her. And I did it all with a few smart Google searches. Not bad! Once you learn how to narrow down the search results and get through the bad ones, the possibilities for finding the information you need are virtually endless.

Of course, there are many Web sites devoted to celebrity addresses, but the big question for you is whether or not the listings are accurate. A Web site of celebrity addresses set up by an autograph collector—but never updated— won't do you any good. Celebrities change agents and managers often, so addresses must be constantly researched and updated.

My service, **Contact Any Celebrity** (www.ContactAnyCelebrity.com) maintains an online database for over 54,000 celebrities, with such info as the best mailing address, agent, manager, publicist, production company and charitable cause, and we update this data every day. My staff can also research any special requests you have and will send you a Postage Refund Check if any letters you send are returned to you by the Postal Service.

BetterWhois

If the celebrity you're looking for has an official Web site, check **BetterWhois** (www.BetterWhois.com). Simply type in the domain name of the Web site, and this service will give you the mailing address, phone, fax and email of the administrative contact listed the domain. This way you can write the celebrity c/o (care of) the administrative contact listed with BetterWhois.

Online Newsgroups & Forums

Internet newsgroups have become a bit of a joke lately, since many are filled with spam advertisements. However, they can still be great places to find specific information, especially when it comes to connecting with other fans regarding a particular celebrity, finding tidbits about the star, and learning how to contact this famous individual.

"Newsgroups" (also called "Usenet") is a part of the Internet in which groups are created for every conceivable topic. People who access those groups can read messages posted by other people or post their own in order to discuss a particular topic. These groups can be very eclectic, ranging from people who like to photograph horses to people who like midget gymnastics, plus everything in between. Therefore, you'll have no trouble finding groups for fans of a specific celebrity with whom you can gossip about the star as much as you want.

Subscribing to a newsgroup is easy once you know how. There's no cost involved, and your browser software can probably handle the job without needing any extra downloads or installations. On the other hand, there are programs that can make organizing the information you find in newsgroups much easier. These are called "news readers" or "newsgroup readers," and they can be found with a simple search on Google for links to some free downloads. If you want to read messages and search the newsgroups for specific information, this **Google Groups** section (groups.google.com) is by far the best way to go.

At groups.google.com, simply enter a search string in the box provided and click the search option. In fact, I did this while writing the earlier section of this book about using our phrase: Julianne Moore contact details. As a result, I found a newsgroup newsletter posting that listed her contact address alongside every other celebrity from the film *Far from Heaven*, which was released in November 2002.

There are literally hundreds of thousands of posts on Usenet. Yet what makes the Google service special is that they have every newsgroup post in their system, all the way back to 1994! Most people don't need to view all those millions of postings from the last 12 years, but that's exactly what Google has done for you.

If you do decide to access a newsgroup, whether it's with a software program or an online service like Google, do not put your email address in the post in an easy-to-read way. If you do, your address will most likely be spammed within days of its first appearance on the newsgroup. Instead, put something like "info at contactanycelebrity dot com" or "info@nospamplease.contactanycelebrity.com" instead. When spammers send their scanners, or spiders, out to automatically harvest email addresses, yours won't register correctly in their database. Anyone who wants to legitimately contact you, however, can do so.

Speaking of spam, it has affected most newsgroups. What you want to look for are "moderated" forums, where a moderator approves every message posted to the newsgroup. That keeps spammers away (for the most part at least). Once you start navigating the various groups, you'll figure out which ones are moderated and which ones aren't much more than a pointless collection of spam.

Industry Resources

You may be a Hilary Duff fan, but did you know that her favorite movie of all time is *Romy and Michele's High School Reunion*, or that she hates techno music, or that she was home-schooled since the age of 10? Probably not, but that sort of info on Duff and background on just about every other celebrity is contained in the **Internet Movie Database (IMDB)** (www.IMDB.com). Simply search for the celebrity you're interested in to check out his or her biography, trivia, the films they were in, the people they're related to, etc.

In addition, every area of the entertainment industry has at least one, if not several, industry trade magazines used by those in the business. In film, TV and music, these resources can be expensive, but single issues are usually sold in your local bookstore like Borders and Barnes & Noble.

Variety (www.Variety.com) is the most instantly recognizable industry newspaper for film and television, and it uses an odd industry lingo that has been around for nearly 100 years. This publication is printed daily, giving us all the inside information on who is starring in what, who is producing what, and who is releasing what. More importantly, it also includes a weekly "production guide" that gives the inside scoop on what is in production. This allows people to write the star they're interested in at the local production company making the movie. So, if Reese Witherspoon is filming a movie or she's about to go on location for a movie in Tennessee, you can try writing the local production company, which will usually forward mail to her once she arrives there.

The Hollywood Reporter (www.HollywoodReporter.com) is an option besides *Variety*, with a similar format and the same information when it comes to production listings. However, it also has good intermittent listings of other information, such as which agencies and management companies represent certain celebrities, who the major power players are, who is getting paid the most, and who are the new actors on the rise to fame. This info on "up and coming stars" is a great tool if you're an autograph collector, because you can write the actors and request an autograph. Since they aren't yet famous, they'll most likely oblige, and you'll know there's a good chance he or she will be a household name in a year or even just a few months.

Billboard (www.Billboard.com) is the music world's version of *Variety*, with industry news and plenty of resources to keep you abreast of who is up and coming in the music biz. Like those mentioned above, this trade resource isn't particularly fan-friendly; however, if you take contacting celebrities seriously, you'll want to start reading and learning as much about the business side of their lives as you can.

Show Business Weekly (SBW) (www.ShowBusinessWeekly.com) is to the live performing arts what *Variety* is to the film world. Every week, *SBW* updates its casting selection news, listing all the important audition and casting notices. In addition, there are in-depth articles for actors. *SBW* may be of limited relevance to anyone not in the acting business. Still, keeping abreast of who is up-and-coming will help you stay on the pulse of the industry if you're an autograph hound or if you're looking to find a screen legend performing up close and personal at a setting near you.

Official Fan Sites

Most celebrities today have lots of unofficial fan sites devoted to them with questionable information, and so many stars have decided to start their own official sites. Sometimes these are very user-friendly. Some are meant to stroke the star's ego, and all you get is a few pictures and a couple of news tidbits now and then. Others are in-depth peeks at what makes the star tick, especially if the celebrity is personally involved in the site.

Ben Affleck used to own www.BenAffleck.com, but he had to shut it down when problems with a network TV pilot forced him to close most of his interactive production company (it is now an unofficial fan site). But when his official site was live, not only did it meticulously catalog every step Affleck took in the world (from archiving newspaper interviews to presenting clips from TV shows), it also had a message board. Ben took great delight in answering questions asked on it. He even called up a few of the regulars, unannounced, just to give them a thrill.

Writer/director Kevin Smith (*Jersey Girl*, *Clerks*, *Dogma*, *Chasing Amy*) has a very fan-friendly Web site at www.ViewAskew.com. Through the site, he not only answers questions from fans, but has also given some of them jobs. He has hosted special events too for correspondents at which he's screened unreleased films from his production company.

For several years on his own Web site, Sir Ian McKellen has been giving his fans information before he gives it to the press at www.McKellen.com. He even kept a running diary while shooting *Lord of the Rings* and shot a home video of the production as well.

Halle Berry's own www.Hallewood.com goes as far as to offer video workout clips, as well as Hally-approved beauty products. Berry's webpages go above and beyond in welcoming fans into her private worlds. Her site has even spawned a group of fans who call themselves "The Groovers," and they communicate with her on a regular basis.

Like the examples above, many other celebrities have made their own official Web sites available to give fans a look into their everyday life. Thousands of celebrities (or their publicists) have taken the time to create a site, and therefore these stars have a link with their fans. Celebrity blogs are also becoming popular, with stars like Rosie O'Donnell (www.Rosie.com) and Moby (www.Moby.com) contributing almost daily posts about their personal lives. Rosie even posts regularly updated videos to her blog using her Web cam!

These examples, however, are far from the norm. Most official celebrity Web sites are little more than a PR offering or a business-driven corporate site, rather than a serious attempt to connect with fans. For example, David Lynch's Web site (www.DavidLynch.com) charges users for access and offers them unique online series content when they do. Fail to pay and there's not much for you to see.

When Johnny Carson was alive, his site said, "Wrong, Johnny won't read your email, but someone from Carson Productions will." Then they offered a series of tapes and DVDs to purchase.

Other official star sites combine commercial and non-commercialism. Madonna's official site (www.Madonna.com) offers free streaming music and music videos, with the option to join her official fan club for instant access to exclusive remixes, autograph giveaways, a newsletter (which is actually a very well-produced magazine), interviews with dancers, artists and photographers who work with her, and more.

For those involved in film and television, there's no better resource for finding official Web sites than the **Internet Movie Database (IMDB)** (www.IMDB.com) which allows you to search for the names of anyone ever involved in film or television. If an official Web site for that celebrity exists, it will usually list it right there, free of charge.

Of course, you can always do a search on Google—for "celebrity name" + "official site." However, this will only show accurate results if the celebrity's site is titled an "official site." Usually it will bring up hundreds of fan sites instead, so it's best to check a resource like www.IMDB.com where the celebrity's personal assistant or publicist has listed the celebrity's actual official site.

If one particular celebrity is the object of your interest, consider starting your own unofficial Web site devoted to that person. Many fans have done this and ended up in close contact with the celebrity once the star (or the star's publicist) realized the unofficial site served a valuable purpose, especially if a lot of people visit it.

Unofficial Fan Sites

Just as the official fan sites can be great places to research celebrities' interests, their unofficial fan sites can be even better. Sometimes the info you'll get from an unofficial site will be more in-depth and personal than what you'd find at the star's official site. This is because often all of the information found on official sites is screened by the star's publicist, and they don't want a lot of info to be made public. The people who run unofficial sites tend to know a lot about their favorite celebrity.

Fan Clubs

Every celebrity with a decent amount of fans has a fan club, and more so with the music industry than any other field of entertainment. If you're interested in contacting a musical artist, the fan club mentioned on the liner notes of one of his or her CDs is a good place to start. Of course, if you download music instead of buying it, you can't read the liner notes, can you? (Unless you legally download music at **iTunes** (www.iTunes.com), which does include liner notes.)

Any official fan club will have access to its celebrity, but that doesn't mean the star will show up for its gatherings or hang out with fan club members on a Friday night. What is does mean is if you join for a price, you're guaranteed to get a signed picture, maybe a t-shirt, a membership card, preferred seating at concerts, and a newsletter. For the diehard fan, the cost is generally not a big deal since the newsletters will give you information on exactly where you can meet your favorite celebrity. Maybe they'll be at a book-signing in Savannah, Georgia this week or a charity event in Saskatoon, Canada next week. That newsletter will usually tell you where and when.

Most fan clubs also have giveaways every so often for backstage passes, front row concert tickets, meet and greets, sound checks, and autographed memorabilia. So a great way to score some cool stuff is becoming a member of a fan club for one of your favorite stars and entering their contests. (I won two free tickets to Madonna's "Drowned World Tour" through her fan club—worth $500 since the tickets were $250 each—and hard to get!).

Admittedly, not every fan club is professionally run and operated. In the 60s and 70s, fan clubs were a huge deal, and they were a substantial business for those who ran them. Nowadays, however, mostly due to the Internet, things are more casual. There are a lot of free online fan clubs with no charge for membership and no real return other than regular news and updates.

There are also plenty of places online that claim to be fan clubs, but very few are in the traditional sense where you actually get anything for signing up. Most are merely collections of photos and in-depth news, but if you're interested in seeing what's out there, try using a reputable search engine like Google. Search for the celebrity's name in quotation marks and the words: fan club.

For example, if you're looking for Madonna's fan club, type in: "Madonna" fan club. The Web site address is usually the name of the celebrity plus .com—for example, hers is www.Madonna.com. Easy, right? Oprah's site at www.Oprah.com invites you to sign up for a free membership and "become part of Oprah's world." Yeah, right . . . if only it were that easy!

For the music fan, thousands of these fan clubs are listed and housed at **Music Fan Clubs** (www.MusicFanClubs.org). Some of them are very professional with lots of info (which wouldn't hurt you to know if you ever do meet the celebrity), but most don't offer any contact information.

To actually contact a celebrity and get a response, you'll probably have to skip fan clubs and instead send a letter to his or her mailing address. For the best mailing addresses for over 54,000 celebrities, you can join my service, **Contact Any Celebrity** (www.ContactAnyCelebity.com), for instant access to my exclusive online database.

Libraries

If you can't find the information you're looking for online, you may have to resort to using the library. Your public library can be a great place to find info on the celebrity you'd like to contact. Librarians do a lot more than only check books in and out. They also research and catalog information, store newspapers and magazines in their archives, and help library patrons find the information they're looking for.

Many libraries subscribe to a database such as **LexisNexis** (www.LexisNexis.com), which catalogs news articles, speeches, official biographical information, and much more. The library will usually allow you to use this service for your own needs, whether it's for a school paper or a fascination with "that guy on that show." Other libraries will allow you to access these resources only if the librarian is searching for you.

The best thing about using a public library for research is that it's not going to cost you much money. You may have to spend a few cents to use the photocopy machine or print pages from the computer, but using a library is often free—thanks to taxpayers like us!

Often the library will store info from old newspapers and pictures in microfiche form, which means it is printed in tiny writing on small strips of microfilm that you view using a large display screen. The screen magnifies the film many times so you can read it like a newspaper, allowing the library to store decades of newspapers and magazines in a single drawer. When your online searching continually comes up with newspapers wanting you to pay for access to an archive, the library makes for a cheaper, albeit more time-consuming alternative.

While at the library, you'll have access to a number of ways to do your own research. This includes the use of *Marquis Who's Who* (www.MarquisWhosWho.com), a collection of extensive biographically based resources—based on regions of

U.S. and the world, business focus (art, politics, science), and more. It's all there for you to use for free, so you might as well do so. You'll find background on the Internet-based Who's Who in the next section, "General Sources."

When in doubt, ask. Librarians will help you find an address if it's available, and they enjoy encouraging you to frequent the library for reading and research. If they can't help you find the info, chances are they'll know someone who can, so go get your library card today!

To find a local library near you, visit the following library resources:

American Library Association
www.ALA.org

Public Library Association
www.PLA.org

General Sources

One of the great research tools for background information about celebrities are the *Marquis Who's Who* listings (www.MarquisWhosWho.com) on the Internet. Marquis has been around since 1899 and now has more than 1.3 million biographies in their database, making it an incredible research tool. This resource is better for finding contact information for public figures like world leaders, religious figures, politicians, etc., than actors and actresses.

When you subscribe to Marquis, you can simply type in a name you're researching and their database will give you the person's background, education, civic service records, family information, awards, affiliations, where they worked, what they've created or achieved, degrees, hobbies, interests, religion, and much more. It incorporates all the information found in the following publications:

- *Who's Who in America*
- *Who Was Who in America*
- *Who's Who in 20th Century America*
- *Who's Who in the World*
- *Who's Who in the East, West, Midwest, South and Southwest*

- *Who's Who of American Women*
- *Who's Who in Science and Engineering*
- *Who's Who in Medicine and Healthcare*
- *Who's Who in Finance and Business*
- *Who's Who in American Law*
- *Who's Who in American Politics*
- *Who's Who in American Art*
- *Who's Who in American Education*
- *Who's Who in American History*
- *Who's Who on the Web*

If you don't want to pay for an online subscription, call your local library and ask if they have an account. As mentioned earlier, many libraries have subscriptions to services like this one and others like LexisNexis that really come in handy when you're digging up contact information.

THREE

Contacting Celebrities on MySpace

"I won't be happy until I'm as famous as God."

—MADONNA

According to a recent Nielsen/NetRatings survey, 60 million+ people visited **MySpace** (www.myspace.com) in August 2007. So what makes MySpace so popular? First, it lets users create their own free profile, including photos, videos, and music. Users can also completely customize the layout, colors, and text of their profiles, adding blogs, event announcements, bulletin posts, and more.

Celebrities know the benefits of being on MySpace. One advantage is that when they make a post to their MySpace blog–talking, for instance, about something they're working on or announcing an event such as a live appearance or autograph signing—their messages will be viewed directly by their fans without having to rely on email lists, spend a lot of money on advertising, etc. Also, other mediums may or may not get their message out in time.

MySpace—The Basics

Extremely popular with teens and young adults, MySpace is part of a growing new trend on the Internet of social networking sites. Although there are many social networking sites online today including **Facebook** (www.Facebook.com), **Friendster** (www.Friendster.com), **Xanga** (www.Xanga.com) and **Ning** (www.Ning.com), MySpace is the most popular. It also has the most celebrities as real members. MySpace is so popular, in fact, that News Corp. bought it for $580 million in 2005! In its latest fiscal year, the company's Fox Interactive unit, consisting largely of MySpace, brought in $550 million—almost matching that investment.

To use MySpace, first you set up your profile. Then you invite your friends to link their profiles to yours and that's when the fun begins! Most of the people linking to you and to your friends will have the same interests, live in the same town, etc. So it's a great way to keep in touch with old friends and also make new ones, which is why MySpace is called a "social networking" site. Think of it like six degrees of separation (but in actuality it's more like three degrees online!).

Although MySpace is currently used mostly by teens, more young adults and adults are signing up every day (including celebrities). So despite what you may have heard about old men setting up profiles on MySpace to lure young children, most people use it to keep in touch with old friends, meet other people like themselves, and to make new friends. You can search for people by zip code, city, high school, college, category of interest (Madonna, soccer, marketing, etc.), and more. This lets you find other people you already know or would like to meet, because they share either the same background or the same interests, career, or hobbies that you do.

MySpace allows its users to share intimate details about their life (sometimes a little too intimate!) that you would perhaps never learn without it since most people put on airs in person. As society becomes more and more socially cut off with technological advances like caller ID, email, and text messages, people are now looking for more and more ways to connect on a personal level while still utilizing "cool" technology. MySpace lets them do just that, and celebrities are no exception. They can now communicate with their fans without having to give out their personal information. Now when they meet their fans they can say, "Look me up on MySpace and send me a message!"

Celebrities on MySpace

Larger-than-life celebrities use MySpace to promote themselves. Madonna, for instance, posts news about her latest album releases, song downloads, screen savers, and more on her profile (www.myspace.com/madonna). Recently it linked to MTV.com so fans could vote for her in the five MTV Video Music Awards categories she was nominated for. Celebrities like Madonna make no qualms about using MySpace as a savvy marketing and promotional tool.

Many celebrities actually set up their profiles themselves, read their messages, and respond to fans directly. Janice Dickinson, the former "love her or hate her" judge on *America's Next Top Model* has her own profile (www.myspace.com/janicedickinsonmodels). She used it to announce casting calls for her reality show the *Janice Dickinson Modeling Agency* on Oxygen. Adult star Jenna Jameson uses her profile (www.myspace.com/jennajameson) to blog about her life and show off photos of herself with stars like Paris Hilton. (Of course, Paris has her own profile (www.myspace.com/parishilton) with sister Nikki Hilton as one of her friends as well). An assistant for Kathy Griffin got hired because she sent a message to Kathy's MySpace profile (www.myspace.com/teamkathygriffin). The woman explained that she was looking to get into the entertainment industry as an assistant, and it just so happened Kathy was looking to hire one!

So how do you know if the celebrity's profile is real or not? (Unfortunately, there are many celebrity imposters—also known as "fakers"—on MySpace.) There are three main ways to tell: number of friends, personal photos, and the profile's design. Usually, the celebrity's profile with the most friends is the official one. For example, if there are two profiles for Madonna, and one has 30,000 friends and the other has 48 friends, you can bet the one with 30,000 friends is hers. (As of this writing, her official profile has 39,386 friends.)

The second way to tell is if the celebrity's profile includes any personal and/or candid photos. (You usually have to have your own profile in order to view photos, so you'll need to create one on MySpace first [see below].) Imposters usually don't have personal photos of the celebrity. The third main way to tell if a celebrity's profile is real is how professionally the profile is designed. MySpace knows that celebrity profiles bring in a lot of users, so they work to make sure the celebrity's profile is customized and professional. Imposter profiles will not look as slick.

Creating Your Own Page & Making the Connection

To set up your own MySpace profile, visit www.MySpace.com and click on Sign Up in the top right-hand corner. From there, fill out the information it asks for and follow the rest of the instructions. After you've set up your profile, you can download profile templates from sites like **MyGen** (www.MyGen.com.uk). Do a search on Google for "myspace profile templates" to find other similar sites.

After you've set up your own MySpace profile, you can send private messages to celebrities you find after you add them as friends. Since most celebrities understand that when you add them as friends to your profile they may gain additional fans among your friends, they'll usually approve your friend request even though they don't know you. As a friend, you can also submit a posting for their page which includes your comments and picture. In addition, a great way to request a free autographed photo from the star is to send a message to them via their page on MySpace, making sure to include your name and address with what you write.

Part Two

. . . .

Tips for Contacting
Certain Types of Celebrities

chapter FOUR

Actors & Actresses

*"Fame is being asked to sign your autograph
on the back of a cigarette packet."*

—BILLY CONNOLLY

Official Channels

Sometimes the reason you may need to contact a celebrity isn't because you want to get to know the celebrity personally. Instead, you might have a business opportunity or charitable cause that could use the star's assistance. These days, you'd need to take the offer through a process that is professional and official.

Nobody is going to sign on to help a superstar charitable organization if its representative is approaching celebrities for help in restaurants while the stars are brunching on eggs Benedict. Likewise, if you're sending away for signed photos with a note that says, "I've got a great opportunity for you. Call me at this number . . . ," you're not going to get very far in getting support from a star.

However, there are channels you can go through, and this chapter describes various ways you can make the right kind of contact with a star.

Screen Actors Guild of America (SAG)

The **Screen Actors Guild** (also known as SAG) has a free telephone hotline available for those who need to find the agent for an actor or actress. They only give the agency name and phone number for up to three celebrities at a time, so if you want more you'll have to call back. The **Actors to Locate Line** is 323–549–6737.

Since it's a free service, the hold times are usually quite long, and often the celebrity's info you're looking for will show up with "no contact information listed." That means you'll have a lot more work to do in order to find the information you want.

To contact the Screen Actors Guild for other reasons, use the following information:

SAG West Coast Office (Hollywood)
5757 Wilshire Boulevard, 7th Floor
Los Angeles, CA 90036–3600
323-954-1600
www.SAG.org

SAG East Coast Office (New York)
360 Madison Avenue, 12th Floor
New York, NY 10017
212-944-1030
www.SAG.org

Visit **Contact Any Celebrity** (www.ContactAnyCelebrity.com) to get the direct mailing addresses for over 9,697 actors and actresses.

Television Show Tapings

Celebrities can be the most accessible, oddly enough, when they're at work. If you're a Jon Stewart fan and you show up at his favorite deli while he's eating lunch, chances are you're probably going to disturb him. But if you get tickets to a taping of *The Daily Show* (which he hosts in New York City), your chance of shaking his hand and getting him to sign something is much better.

The stars who work in live television depend on the audience to help them do their job. With sitcoms, for example, the audience may provide the entire laugh track, and some shows like *Scrubs* and *30 Rock* have this as their official policy. If the audience doesn't laugh at a joke, the writers will scramble to modify it or come up with a new one. So when you watch a television sitcom like *Scrubs*, you're hearing the actual audience that was at the taping that day laugh throughout the entire show. For late night shows like Stewart's, the hosts need you to laugh at their jokes because it helps them project enthusiasm for national TV. And on talk shows like *Ellen* and *Oprah*, the host and producers need to be able to feel out the audience like the sitcoms do so they know what's working or not working.

Most TV shows that have a live audience also have a "warm-up guy" whose job is to tell a few jokes, lay out the ground rules, maybe do some audience participation, and get everyone in the studio totally warmed up for the show. If there's a delay or a break in shooting, this guy has to keep things going so the audience doesn't get bored and want to leave. He's also your best bet to get to the on-screen talent and sometimes will even bring a star up to the audience section.

Regarding this celebrity exposure, some stars do hang around after and talk to audience members one-on-one. Some won't, but the warm-up guy will talk to anyone. So if you can make him feel important, he can quite often help you get to the people you really want to meet.

Don't ask one of the producers if you can go backstage—they'll say no. Don't ask an intern to get something signed—you'll get a "no" there too. But that warm-up guy is usually working so hard (and is maybe even a little annoyed that he's not the star of the show) that you can sometimes get him to do you a favor if you play your cards right.

TV show taping tickets do not cost money, except for special circumstances like concerts, awards shows, and sporting events. Sitcom tapings and game shows are free of charge. Often the audience will be much smaller than you expected (*The Daily Show* seats 100 people), while half the audience noise in a *Wheel of Fortune* taping is from the crew itself.

The peak television production season is generally August through March for most of the major networks. These include ABC, CBS, FOX, NBC, UPN, WB, TNN, the Disney Channel and Nickelodeon. Situation comedies, reality, and game shows are the ones most likely to require a live audience, since dramas don't require audience interaction.

Remember that a TV show taping is not a quick prospect. You're not only there for the half hour you see during the final product. You have to be there early, you must sit around while they set up, and you're required to go through the warm-up. Then the cast will probably do one rehearsal from start to finish, and they will film several takes for each scene so the editors have plenty of options. All of this can take a long time, even up to eight hours (I know this from personal experience!). Plus they're not going to serve lunch or dinner partway through. Of course, the actors can eat all they want from the catering table backstage, and they often come out on stage with food to rub in the fact that they're eating and you can't. But it's still fun. Just make sure to eat before you go in, use the restroom before you take your seat, and turn off your cell phone.

Often the funniest part of a live TV taping isn't the acting itself, it's what goes on behind the scenes. If an actor is making a joke, the actors off camera will often react to what he or she is saying in an unexpected way. People will crack up, others will adlib, and shots will get messed up and have to be re-taped. It's an interesting look at what goes on behind the scenes of television, even if you don't get to meet the star of the show.

To get a ticket, see the resources below. You normally have to make reservations for popular shows months in advance because they fill up quickly. If all else fails, you can sometimes find studio workers handing out tickets in front of Grauman's Chinese Theater at 6925 Hollywood Boulevard (where the famous handprints are) and in front of the Hollywood Boulevard and Highland Avenue shopping complex next door toward the east.

Once you have your ticket, the rules are simple—applaud when you're told to, laugh when you think something is funny, don't yell out at random times, don't curse, don't disrupt other people around you, stay seated until the end of the show (restroom breaks come before the show, not during), and don't take photographs.

Remember, if a scene has to be redone, you're going to have to laugh all over again. The truth is that the show taping isn't about your entertainment. It is about your assistance in putting together a good show. If you get bored easily by repetition or sitting for a long period of time, attending a live TV taping probably isn't for you. On the other hand, if you enjoy watching how television shows are created and you don't mind following the rules, you'll have a lot of fun, learn a lot, and maybe even get to meet or at least watch a favorite star.

To Attend TV Show Tapings

ABC Network Live Shows

www.abc.go.com/site/tvtickets.html

Audiences for most ABC shows are handled by outside entities, but you can be directed to the people you need to talk to via the Web site above.

CBS Network Live Shows

212-975-2476 (New York)
323-575-2458 (Los Angeles)
www.CBS.com

To get tickets for a CBS show by mail, send a self-addressed stamped envelope:

CBS Tickets
7800 Beverly Boulevard
Los Angeles, CA 90036

NBC Network Live Shows

212-664-3056 (New York)
818-954-6000 (Los Angeles)
www.nbc.com/nbc/footer/tickets.shtml

Tickets for most NBC shows with a live audience are not available through NBC. You can, however, find tickets for many of their shows at www.TVTickets.com, which is run by Audiences Unlimited, Inc. and isn't affiliated with NBC.

To Attend TV Show Tapings in Los Angeles

Audience Associates
323-467-4697 or 818-985-8811
www.TVTix.com
tvtix@tvtix.com or groups@tvtix.com

Audience Associates regularly recruits for crowd scenes in movies. Web site reservations are given the highest priority.

Audiences Unlimited
100 Universal City Plaza
Universal City, CA 91608
818-753-3470, ext. 321
www.TVTickets.com
tickets@audiencesunlimited.com

The Audiences Unlimited Web site includes schedules for shows, pilots and specials, show changes, studio maps and more.

CBS Studio City Tickets
7800 Beverly Boulevard
Los Angeles, CA 90036
323-575-2458

Free tickets to live tapings of CBS TV shows can be acquired at CBS's ticket window on the west side of CBS TV City which faces Fairfax. The ticket window is open Monday through Friday from 7:30 A.M. to 5:00 p.m., although it is sometimes open on the weekend if a show is being taped. For tickets by mail, send a self-addressed stamped envelope to the address above.

HollywoodTickets.com
818-688-3974
www.HollywoodTickets.com
tickets@hollywoodtickets.com

HollywoodTickets.com allows you to print your own TV taping tickets from their website, and you can also browse TV taping line-ups so you can find the best shows to fit your schedule.

To Attend TV Show Tapings in New York City

Saturday Night Live

Advance ticket requests are only handled in August and are given out in a lottery system. Send an email to snltickets@nbcuni.com with your name, address and phone number. If you are selected, you will be given two tickets for a random date and time.

Standby tickets are available at 7:00 A.M. every Saturday that shows are taped on the 49th Street side of 30 Rockefeller Plaza. They are given on a first-come, first-served basis and are strictly limited to one per person. You may get a ticket for the 8 p.m. dress rehearsal or the 11:30 p.m. live taping.

Total Request Live (TRL)

To get tickets ahead of time for the show, email tricasting@mtvstaff.com. Alternatively, try getting a standby ticket by arriving at 2:00 p.m. or earlier at MTV Studios, 1515 Broadway between 43rd and 44th Streets. Young adults between the ages of 18 and 24 are preferred by the producers.

To Attend Shows in the U.K.

BBC

The BBC is always looking for people to take an active part in their game shows, comedy audiences, and even documentaries. More info can be found at www.bbc.co.uk/whatson/beonashow. For free tickets to BBC TV and radio shows, go to www.bbc.co.uk/whatson/tickets.

TV Recordings

www.TVRecordings.com

If it's shot in London, you can probably get tickets at this Web site. Registration is required.

BeOn Screen

www.BeOnScreen.com

BeOnScreen.com is a resource for potential U.K. TV guests, show participants, and audience members. Search BeOn's directory of TV programs and register for email updates. This site is also used by TV producers who often place ads for their projects on this site.

More TV Show Taping Resources

Studio Audiences

www.StudioAudiences.com

This Web site brings info from many other sites together in one place. You can find the contact information for just about any show right here.

On Camera Audiences

www.OCATV.com

On Camera coordinates tickets for TV programs all across the country. Shows include the Late, *Late Show with Craig Ferguson* and *Family Feud*, which are both shot in the LA area.

New York TV Show Tickets, Inc.

www.NYTix.com

They list New York television shows as well as discount Broadway tickets, starving artist tickets, secret discount codes, and city tours.

Television Exhibitions, Conferences & Conventions

Every year, the television industry holds a large number of events where it unveils its new shows to the media, hypes upcoming projects, gets the press talking, and generally wines and dines anyone who can help them over the next business year. Getting into these conventions is quite a feat. However, once you're in, you'll have access to many people you otherwise wouldn't be able to get near.

Some conventions require nothing more than a registration fee and are open to the general public. But those that are held for industry people only, which most of them tend to be, can sometimes get costly. Of course, there's always a way around that! The first way is to become a member of the organization running a convention. For example, the **NATPE (National Association of Television Programming Executives)** has a convention each year that attracts a few headliners, and members receive a discount on their registration. Another way is to obtain credentials as a member of the media, although this takes a little more planning, effort, and patience. You'll find more info on this in the "Musicians" chapter.

The most important thing to remember when attending a TV convention is to do it the right way—don't gush over the stars and don't run around like a maniac grabbing every autograph you can. If a security guard sees the panic of an autograph hound in your eyes and starts asking questions, you could be on your way out the door. Chill out, act like an executive, and know your story.

There are literally dozens of TV conventions every year that attract celebrities, but more often than not they won't tell you ahead of time who is going to be there. However, if Jessica Biel is headlining a new series on CBS, chances are she'll show up at the next big television convention to hype the series. Still there are no guarantees.

Some conventions to keep an eye out for include:

MIPTV (International Audiovisual Content Trade Show)—Cannes, France

This one takes place during the Cannes Film Festival, which makes it prime ground for celebrity spotting. Nearly every television station and distributor in the world will be represented by their buyers, development execs and, of course, celebrities. About 12,000 attendees were there in 2007.

MIPTV (France)
www.MIPTV.com

NATPE (National Association of Television Programming Executives)— Las Vegas

The National Association of Television Programming Executive events are important ones for those in the biz. This is a global organization so its conferences extended beyond those offered in the United States. Its main annual conference is held in Las Vegas.

NATPE Headquarters
www.NATPE.org

Film Festivals

Some of the best places to spot celebrities in one place without tons of security, assistants, and people keeping you away is at a film festival. Every week, all over the world, film festivals take place that allow fans and people in the industry the opportunity to watch indie (independent) films looking for release, studio films trying to build audience buzz ahead of their release, and international films you might not otherwise get the chance to see at all.

One of the fringe benefits of these events is that the festivals often bring the stars and director of the movie out either before or after the screening to answer questions from fans. These folks also appear at parties and accept awards at the festivities. Some festivals are too small to attract much in the way of celebrities, like the Cleveland Film Festival, while others work hard to draw in two or three big names. Of course, the most well-known film festivals, like Sundance, Cannes, Toronto, and Tribeca, are always crawling with celebs.

There are two main ways to meet celebrities at these events. The first is to actually buy a ticket and hope for the best. The second is to attempt to get into the industry parties, where you could be a lot more successful. Celebrities often let their hair down at a film festival, but only when they're in their own crowd. At a party for industry players, a celebrity will mingle, chat, give out contact info, talk about things they normally wouldn't, and generally be themselves. If you're a producer, a lawyer, an accountant, or a journalist, then you're more than welcome to come to such an affair—just as long as you specialize in the entertainment industry. If you're not yet a player in the "industry," you'll need to get a little more creative.

The first thing the creative will need is a *good* business card. Get a friend who knows his or her way around graphic design programs like PhotoShop, InDesign, or Quark to make you something that looks professional, corporate, full-color, and instantly credible. Word your title as impressively as possible, even though you may only be working for yourself at this point. You get the idea.

The next thing you need is an industry pass, which is like a season ticket for a film festival. You get your picture taken, and then you get a laminated pass that hangs around your neck and announces to the world that "Walter J. Smith" is a credible industry type. Usually you have to show your business card at registration, fill out a form, and pay the admission fee to get one. Then you start asking around whether there are any parties going on. Most film festivals have a detailed Web site that will tell you how to register and get on board.

One last piece of advice: Film festivals are *not* the place to ask for a photo or an autograph. Industry people just don't do that. If you do, you'll likely be politely escorted away and asked not to return.

Here are some of the top film festivals worth exploring:

Major Film Festivals

Aspen Filmfest
110 E. Hallam, #102
Aspen, CO 81611
970-925-6882 (Phone)
970-925-1967 (Fax)
filmfest@aspenfilm.org
www.aspenfilm.org

Atlanta Film Festival
IMAGE Film & Video Center
535 Means Street NW, #C
Atlanta, GA 30318
404-352-4225 (Phone)
404-352-0173 (Fax)
aff@imagefv.org
www.atlantafilmfestival.com/

Austin Film Festival
1604 Nueces Street
Austin, TX 78701
512-478-4795, 1-800-310-FEST (Phone)
512-478-6205 (Fax)
info@austinfilmfestival.com
www.austinfilmfestival.com

Beverly Hills Film Festival
9663 Santa Monica Boulevard, #777
Beverly Hills, CA 90210
310-779-1206 (Phone)
mail@beverlyhillsfilmfestival.com
www.beverlyhillsfilmfestival.com

Cannes International Film Festival
3 rue Amelie
Paris, 75007
FRANCE
33-(0)-1-53-59-61-00 (Phone)
33-(0)-1-53-59-61-10 (Fax)
festival@festival-cannes.fr
www.festival-cannes.org

Fort Lauderdale International Film Festival
1314 E. Las Olas, #007
Fort Lauderdale, FL 33301
954-760-9898 (Phone)
954-760-9099 (Fax)
info@fliff.com
www.fliff.com

Hawaii International Film Festival
680 Iwilei Road, Suite 100
Honolulu, HI 96817 USA
808-528-3456 (Phone)
808-536-2707 (Fax)
info@hiff.org
www.hiff.org

Hollywood Film Festival
433 N. Camden Drive, #600
Beverly Hills, CA 90210
310-288-1882 (Phone)
310-288-0060 (Fax)
awards@hollywoodawards.com
www.hollywoodawards.com

Miami Gay & Lesbian Film Festival
1521 Alton Road, #147
Miami Beach, FL 33139
305-534-9924 (Phone)
305-535-2377 (Fax)
info@mglff.com
www.mglff.com

Miami International Film Festival
c/o Miami Dade College
25 NE 2nd Street, Floor 5501
Miami, FL 33132
305-237-FILM (Phone)
305-237-7344 (Fax)
info@miamifilmfestival.com
www.miamifilmfestival.com

New York Film Festival
70 Lincoln Center Plaza
New York, NY 10023-6569
212-875-5638 (Phone)
212-875-5636 (Fax)
festival@filmlinc.com
www.filmlinc.com

Palm Beach International Film Festival
289 Via Naranjas, #48
Boca Raton, FL 33432
561-362-0003 (Phone)
561-362-0035 (Fax)
info@pbifilmfest.org
www.pbifilmfest.org

Palm Springs International Film Festival
1700 E. Tahquitz Canyon Way, #3
Palm Springs, CA 92262
760-322-2930 (Phone)
760-322-4087 (Fax)
info@psfilmfest.org
www.psifilmfest.org

San Diego Latino Film Festival
921 25th Street
San Diego, CA 92102
619-230-1938 (Phone)
619-230-1937 (Fax)
sdlff@sdlatinofilm.com
www.sdlatinofilm.com

Santa Barbara International Film Festival
1528 Chapala Street, #203
Santa Barbara, CA 93103
805-963-0023 (Phone)
805-962-2524 (Fax)
info@sbfilmfestival.org
www.sbfilmfestival.org

Seattle International Film Festival
400 9th Avenue North
Seattle, WA 98109
206-464-5840 (Phone)
206-264-7919 (Fax)
info@seattlefilm.org
www.seattlefilm.org

Sundance Film Festival
8530 Wilshire Blvd., 3rd Floor
Beverly Hills, CA 90211-3114
310-360-1981 (Phone)
310-360-1969 (Fax)
la@sundance.org
www.sundance.org

chapter
FIVE

Musicians & Music Groups

"It's definitely a dream come true, to be
recognized and to be able to sign autographs."

—CHRISTINA AGUILERA

On the Road

If the celebrity you want is a musical artist or an entire band, your chances of a face-to-face encounter are much better at a live show than elsewhere. That is, as long as you're prepared to do some waiting around, fast-talking, or advance planning.

There are three good options when you're staking out a live show:

Option 1. Waiting at the stage door and grabbing a quick word as they move through, either in or out.

Option 2. Talk your way backstage, where you can mingle with the special people.

Option 3. Call ahead, and spin a tale that you're a special person and need to have your backstage passes waiting.

Option 1: The Stage Door

This is the preferred method for cheapskates everywhere, because you don't need a ticket to wait at the stage door. You simply find out where the artist or group you're interested in is playing, locate the stage door, then wait . . . and wait . . . and wait. Sweet-talking a security guard or two (if you can pull it off) won't hurt either.

Every concert venue has a back door where the talent enters and leaves. Understand that you're probably not the only one who will be waiting, and that quite often the talent will stay backstage for an hour or longer after a show, hanging out with VIPs, getting drunk (or worse), showering, and recuperating. Meanwhile you're outside waiting in the cold for them to appear for three seconds on the way out to the tour bus. But if you can handle the wait, you're likely to find success using this method.

When they do come out, if there's any sort of a crowd waiting, there will likely be a surge to get their attention. A nice musician will deal with that well, stopping to talk to everyone and giving you their time. However, most musicians simply aren't "that nice." They're busy people, tired people, annoyed people, and temperamental people who just want to get back to their hotel room, the after-party, or the house where someone has a huge supply of cocaine. I'm just saying.

In most celebrity contact situations, it pays to be the nice fan with a cool conversation intro and a patient sensibility. But here you'll be competing for space with a crowd of admirers, all desperate to touch their idol. You really need to throw conventional behavior out the window and start pushing your way out to the front.

Be prepared, have something to sign and a way for them to sign it, and most importantly, accept it with a smile. If they only have time to wave and move out . . . that's life.

Option 2: Talking Your Way Backstage

It may seem a little sexist to say so, but if you're a guy, you've got next to no chance of getting backstage for a concert (unless you're a member of the media or industry or just so damn cool that people can't say no to you). Women, especially attractive women, find it much easier to convince security guards, roadies, and venue staff that they should be allowed backstage, simply because rock stars like attractive women. They usually like many attractive women at once, but that's a whole other book.

There's really no great secret to making this method work. You're either physically equipped for it or you're not. Sure, someone with a real gift of the gab can possibly come up with some reason to get backstage, but that's a BIG if.

However, you might as well give it a try—everyone else will—and if you do manage to get access backstage, you must remember three golden rules:

1. Don't stare. Move around and mingle, first with the employees (roadies and the like), then the backup band, and then once you've made "friends" with people, you have a reason to be there and can actually approach the star.

2. Don't gush. A single "Oh wow, it's him!" can kill your routine in a second and see you escorted out.

3. Don't get in the way. If you annoy a roadie, he'll generally not hold back in demonstrating that annoyance.

Option 3: Advance Groundwork

The hard fact is that the media has access to celebrities that common people will never get. When journalists call up a venue and say they're coming to the Celine Dion concert that night, they can expect seat upgrades, access to the press area, access to the talent, and much more depending on the level of fame of the person in the show. Some bands are totally happy to have the press around and will invite a journalist backstage, to the after-party, whatever they want. Others could care less.

So if you have any media connections, it doesn't hurt to use them in this situation. Alternately, some smart people have even created a media outlet for the sole purpose of using that outlet to open doors. A film critic named Paul Fischer is infamous for getting himself invited to film sets all the time to speak with famous actors on the pretense that he will publish the ensuing stories in newspapers, but Fischer was not a regularly employed newspaper journalist.

This is the kind of routine many people in the music industry use to get free CDs, concert tickets, and invitations to parties—they pull a Paul Fischer and either piggyback on small outlets that need free content, or create their very own Web site they will use to open doors—even if nobody actually goes there.

If you're going to go to that extent, you'll have to do a little work up front. You will have to get letterhead printed, invest in a fax machine, change your answering machine or voicemail message to include your company name, and present the image of a professional business overall. But in today's world of blogs and the Internet, it's easier than ever to create your own media outlet and use that to score press passes. Start looking over concert listings in your local paper and online, choose your favorite option above, and push forward.

Away from the Tour

If you need more from a celebrity musician than a handshake, quick conversation, or a backstage share of their recreational drug supply, then you might want to figure out a way to track them down during their time away from the tour. Generally, most famous bands or musicians have the same setup that actors do—a fan club, an assistant who fields their mail, and an agent, manager, or publicist who deals with their business matters.

If you want to offer a celebrity an actual business proposition—such as a charity appearance, a television commercial, or a TV show booking, then you're better off going directly to the agent or record label that handles the artist. Calling the record label often entails a long line of phone calls and getting transferred to other people in the company who will also transfer you to someone else who will eventually say, "He's not in today." That's fine . . . just get a fax number and send your proposal that way. Most of the time you'll get a lot more attention if they think your request is official and not some crazy fan calling up with a pseudo story; a faxed request on official letterhead is best.

If you are a crazy music fan who simply wants to get in touch with the celebrity, then it's best going through the fan club or fan mail address. Sometimes you can find this listed in the liner notes of the musician's CD. You won't acquire some sort of magical insight into the celebrity by doing that, but you'll probably get something—a signed photo or, at the very least, details of how to get a signed photo. From there, simply work your way up. Learn all you can about the celebrity and where he or she is appearing, and hope that they'll fall head over heels in love with you as you sit there in the third row.

Do take caution with musicians, because they tend to pick up a lot of crazed fans when they reach a certain height of fame. They also tend to take a lot of female fans back to the hotel with them. This may seem like a good idea at the time, but almost always ends up with an early morning shove out the door.

Listings of Music Celebrity Fan Clubs

Here's one stop that will give you access to many fan clubs, including ones for Billy Ray Cyrus and the Oak Ridge Boys—the **International Fan Club Organization** (www.ifco.org/fanclubs.htm).

Sending Fan Mail

One way to write to country music celebrities is through the following address. More often than not, they make sure the letter gets into the right hands:

Country Music Television
2806 Opryland Drive
Nashville, TN 37214
www.CMT.com

Besides fan clubs and fan mail addresses, another place to write to musicians is to their record labels.

Visit **Contact Any Celebrity** (www.ContactAnyCelebrity.com) to get the direct mailing addresses of over 3,806 musicians and music groups.

Major Record Label Addresses

A&M Records
2220 Colorado Avenue, Floor 5
Santa Monica, CA 90404
310-865-1000 (Phone)
310-865-7270 (Fax)
firstname.lastname@umusic.com
www.umusic.com

Angel Records
150 Fifth Avenue, Floor 6
New York, NY 10011
212-786-8600 (Phone)
www.angelrecords.com

Arista Associated Labels (LA)
8750 Wilshire Boulevard, Floor 3
Beverly Hills, CA 90211
310-358-4600 (Phone)
310-358-4307 (Fax)
firstname.lastname@bmg.com
www.aristaassociatedlabels.com

Arista Records (NY)
888 Seventh Avenue
New York, NY 10019
212-489-7400 (Phone)
212-830-2124 (Fax)
firstname.lastname@bmg.com
www.arista.com

Arista Records (TN)
1400 18th Ave. South
Nashville, TN 37212
615-301-4488 (Phone)
615-301-4438 (Fax)
info@arista.com
www.aristanashville.com

Artist Direct Records
10900 Wilshire Blvd., #1400
Los Angeles, CA 90024
310-443-5360 (Phone)
310-443-5361 (Fax)
www.artistdirect.com

Atlantic Records (LA)
9229 Sunset Boulevard, #900
Los Angeles, CA 90069
www.atlanticrecords.com

Atlantic Records (NY)
1290 Ave. of the Americas
New York, NY 10104
212-707-2000 (Phone)
212-405-5475 (Fax)
firstname.lastname@atlantic-recordings.com
www.atlantic-records.com

Atlantic Records (LA)
3400 W. Olive
Burbank, CA 91505
8180-238-6800 (Phone)
firstname.lastname@atlantic-recordings.com
www.atlantic-records.com

Bad Boy Entertainment
1710 Broadway
New York, NY 10019
212-381-1540 (Phone)
212-381-1599 (Fax)
firstinitiallastname@badboyworldwide.com
www.badboyonline.com

Blue Note Records
150 Fifth Avenue, Floor 6
New York, NY 10011
212-786-8600 (Phone)
www.bluenote.com

BMG Records/BMG Entertainment
1540 Broadway,
New York, NY 10036
212-930-4000 (Phone)
www.bmg.com

Capitol Records (LA)
1750 N. Vine Street
Los Angeles, CA 90028
323-462-6252 (Phone)
323-467-5267 (Fax)
firstname.lastname@capitolrecords.com
www.capitolrecords.com

Capitol Records (NY)
810 Seventh Avenue
New York, NY 10019
212-253-3000 (Phone)
212-253-3099 (Fax)
firstname.lastname@capitolrecords.com
www.capitolrecords.com

Capitol Records (TN)
3322 W. End Avenue, Floor 11
Nashville, TN 37203
615-269-2000 (Phone)
firstname.lastname@emicap.com
www.capitol-nashville.com

Columbia Records
550 Madison Avenue
New York, NY 10022
212-833-8000 (Phone)
firstname_lastname@sonymusic.com
www.columbiarecords.com

Elektra Entertainment (LA)
2400 W. Olive Street, Floor 2
Burbank, CA 91505
818-238-2200 (Phone)
firstname.lastname@elektra.com
ww.elektra.com

Elektra Entertainment (NY)
75 Rockefeller Plaza
New York, NY 10019
212-275-4000 (Phone)
firstname.lastname@elektra.com
www.elektra.com

Epic Records Group (LA)
2100 Colorado Avenue
Santa Monica, CA 90404
firstname_lastname@sonymusic.com
www.epicrecords.com

Epic Records (NY)
550 Madison Avenue
New York, NY 10022
212-833-8000 (Phone)
firstname_lastname@sonymusic.com
www.epicrecords.com

Epic Records (TN)
34 Music Square East
Nashville, TN 37203
615-742-4379 (Phone)
615-742-4338 (Fax)
http//www.sonynashville.com

Geffen Records
2220 Colorado Avenue, Floor 4
Santa Monica, CA 90404
310-865-4500 (Phone)
310-865-1610 (Fax)
firstname.lastname@umusic.com
www.geffen.com

Hollywood Records (LA)
500 S Buena Vista Street
Burbank, CA 91521
818-560-5670 (Phone)
818-560-3230 (Fax)
firstname.lastname@disney.com
www.hollywoodrecords.com

Hollywood Records (NY)
99 Hudson Street, Floor 8
New York, NY 10013
212-925-0331 (Phone)
212-925-9126 (Fax)
firstname.lastname@disney.com
www.hollywoodrecords.com

The Island Def Jam Music Group, Inc.
825 Eighth Avenue, Floor 28
New York, NY 10019
212-333-8000 (Phone)
212-603-7931 (Fax)
firstname.lastname@umusic.com
www.islanddefjam.com

J Records
745 Fifth Avenue, Floor 6
New York, NY 10151
646-840-5600 (Phone)
646-840-5791 (Fax)
firstname.lastname@bmg.com
www.jrecords.com

Jive Records (LA)
9000 Sunset Blvd., #300
West Hollywood, CA 90069
310-247-8300 (Phone)
310-247-8366 (Fax)
firstname.lastnam@jiverecords.com
www.jiverecords.com

Jive Records (NY)
137-139 W. 25th Street
New York, NY 10001
212-727-0016 (Phone)
212-645-3783 (Fax)
firstname.lastname@jiverecords.com
www.jiverecords.com

Maverick Recording Company
3300 Warner Boulevard
Burbank, CA 91505
818-846-9090 (Phone)
firstname.lastname@maverick.com
www.maverick.com

Mercury Nashville
54 Music Square East, #300
Nashville, TN 37203
615-524-7500 (Phone)
615-524-7600 (Fax)
www.mercurynashville.com

Motown
(See Universal Motown Records Group)

NBC Records, Inc.
3400 W. Olive Avenue, #600
Burbank, CA 91505
818-526-6963 (Phone)
818-526-6946 (Fax)
firstname.lastname@nbc.com
www.nbc.com

RCA Records (LA)
8750 Wilshire Boulevard
Beverly Hills, CA 90211
310-358-4000 (Phone)
310-358-4040 (Fax)
firstname.lastname@bmg.com
www.rcarecords.com

RCA Records (NY)
1540 Broadway
New York, NY 10036
212-930-4000
www.rcarecords.com

RCA Records (TN)
1400 18th Ave. South
Nashville, TN 37212
615-301-4300 (Phone)
615-301-4347 (Fax)
firstname.lastname@bmg.com
www.rcarecords.com

Reprise Records
3300 Warner Boulevard
Burbank, CA 91505
818-846-9090
www.repriserecords.com

Reprise Records (LA)
3300 Warner Blvd.
Burbank, CA 91505
818-846-9090 (Phone)
www.repriserec.com

Reprise Records (NY)
75 Rockefeller Plaza
New York, NY 10019
212-275-4500 (Phone)
212-275-4595 (Fax)
www.repriserec.com

Rhino Records
3400 W. Olive
Burbank, CA 91505
818-238-6200 (Phone)
818-562-9236 (Fax)
www.rhino.com

Shady Records
270 Lafayette, #805
New York, NY 10012
212-324-2410 (Phone)
212-324-2415 (Fax)
www.shadyrecords.com

Sony Music Entertainment (LA)
2100 Colorado Avenue
Santa Monica, CA 90404
310-449-2100 (Phone)
310-449-2959 (Fax)
www.sonymusic.com

Sony Music Entertainment (NY)
550 Madison Avenue
New York, NY 10022
212-833-8000 (Phone)
212-833-4812 (Fax)
www.sonymusic.com

Sony Music Nashville
34 Music Square East
Nashville, TN 37203
615-742-4321 (Phone)
Firstname_lastname@sonymusic.com
www.sonynashville.com

Sony Tropical
605 Lincoln Road, Floor 6
Miami, FL 33139
305-695-3500 (Phone)
305-695-3624 (Fax)
firstname_lastname@sonymusic.com
www.sony.com

Sony Urban (LA)
2100 Colorado Boulevard
Santa Monica, CA 90404
310-449-2100 (Phone)
www.sonyurban.com

Sony Urban (NY)
550 Madison Avenue
New York, NY 10022
212-833-8000
www.sonyurban.com

Tommy Boy Entertainment
32 W. 18th Street, Floor 12
New York, NY 10011
212-388-8300 (Phone)
212-388-8431 (Fax)
firstname.lastname@tommyboy.com
www.tommyboy.com

Universal Motown Records Group
1755 Broadway
New York, NY 10019
212-373-0600 (Phone)
firstname.lastname@umusic.com
www.motown.com

Universal Music Group (LA)
2220 Colorado Avenue
Santa Monica, CA 90404
310-865-5000 (Phone
www.umusic.com

Universal Music Group (NY)
1755 Broadway
New York, NY 10019
212-841-8000 (Phone)
www.umusic.com

Universal Music Group (TN)
54 Music Square East, #300
Nashville, TN 37203
615-524-7500 (Phone)
615-524-7600 (Fax)
firstname.lastname@umusic.com
www.umusic.com

Universal Music Latino (FL)
420 Lincoln Road, #200
Miami Beach, FL 33139
305-938-1300 (Phone)
305-938-1369 (Fax)
firstname.lastname@umusic.com
www.universalmusica.com

Universal Music Latino (LA)
100 N. First Street, Floor 3
Burbank, CA 91502
818-972-5677 (Phone)
818-972-5611 (Fax)
firstname.lastname@umusic.com
www.universalmusica.com

The Verve Music Group (LA)
100 N. First Street, Floor 4
Burbank, CA 91502
818-729-4804 (Phone)
818-729-4904 (Fax)
firstname.lastname@umusic.com
www.veremusicgroup.com

The Verve Music Group (NY)
1755 Broadway, Floor 3
New York, NY 10019
212-331-2000 (Phone)
212-331-2064 (Fax)
firstname.lastname@umusic.com
www.vervemusicgroup.com

Virgin Records America, Inc. (LA)
5750 Wilshire Boulevard
Los Angeles, CA 90036
323-692-1100 (Phone)
www.virginrecords.com

Virgin Records America, Inc. (NY)
150 Fifth Avenue
New York, NY 10010
212-786-8300 (Phone)
www.virgin.com

Warner Bros. Records (LA)
3300 Warner Boulevard
Burbank, CA 91505
818-846-9090 (Phone)
firstname.lastname@wbr.com
www.wbr.com

Warner Bros. Records (NY)
75 Rockefeller Plaza
New York, NY 10019
212-275-4500 (Phone)
firstname.lastname@wbr.com
www.wbr.com

Warner Bros. Records (TN)
20 Music Square East, Floor 3
Nashville, TN 37203
615-748-8000 (Phone)
615-214-1567 (Fax)
firstname.lastname@wbr.com
www.wbrnashville.com

chapter
SIX

Talk Show Hosts

Lisa: *Oprah, can I have your autograph?*
Oprah: *Sure Lisa. Wait a minute, what is this?*
Lisa: *Oh, you're adopting me. It's all
nice and legal, I assure you.*

—THE SIMPSONS

As noted in the "Actors & Actresses" chapter, the best way to meet your favorite celebrity can be as a member of the audience at one of their TV shows. This is true for talk show hosts as well as dramatis performers. To send fan mail to a host, simply write to them at the address for their show.

Below is info on some of today's most popular talk shows:

Chicago

Jerry Springer

Call 312–321–5365 or write:

The Jerry Springer Show
454 N. Columbus Drive, 2nd Floor
Chicago, IL 60611

Or visit www.JerrySpringerTV.com to request tickets via email.

The Oprah Winfrey Show

The Oprah Winfrey Show
110 N. Carpenter Street
Chicago, IL 60607

For *The Oprah Winfrey Show*, reservations are handled "almost exclusively" by phone. Reservations are in high demand. You can encounter busy signals for a long time, and you may even go to the Web site and find that the reservation line has been closed.

However, you usually have to talk to an Audience Department rep (312–633–0808) to get reservations. Sometimes, you might get lucky and be able to request last-minute reservations by email. Stop by Oprah's Web site to check the current status.

Visit www.oprah.com/tows/program/tows_prog_getticks.jhtml.

Los Angeles

Dr. Phil

Dr. Phil
5555 Melrose Avenue
Mae West Building
Los Angeles, CA 90038
Call 323-461-PHIL or visit:
www.drphil.com/shows/page/be_in_the_audience

Ellen

Ellen
3000 W. Alameda Avenue, #2700
Burbank, CA 91523

Visit ellen.warnerbros.com/tickets/ for an online calendar where you can select a date when tickets are available.

The Tonight Show with Jay Leno

The Tonight Show with Jay Leno
3000 W. Alameda Avenue
Burbank, CA 91523

For *The Tonight Show*, send a self-addressed stamped envelope with a brief letter listing the desired date of a taping and three alternate dates. You can request up to four tickets by mail, or try to get tickets on the day of the taping at the NBC Box Office located at the address above. The box office opens at 8 A.M.

To learn more about the show, go to: www.nbc.com/The_Tonight_Show_with_Jay_Leno

New York City

Daily Show with Jon Stewart

Daily Show with Jon Stewart
2049 Century Park East, #4170
Los Angeles, CA 90067

Call 212–586–2477 and tell them how many tickets you need. For more background on the show, visit www.comedycentral.com/shows/the_daily_show/index.jhtml.

Emeril Live

Emeril Live
1180 6th Avenue, Floor 12
New York, NY 10036

The Food Network uses a lottery for tickets due to the high demand, but the sign-up period for the lottery happens only a few times per year. Entry dates are posted on www.FoodTV.com before each lottery period begins. The Food Network will ignore calls, emails, and letters, so don't even try. If your name is picked, a member of the *Emeril Live* staff will notify you by phone two to four weeks before the taping date.

Good Morning America

Good Morning America
ABC Times Square Studios
1500 Broadway
New York, NY 10036

If you want to watch Diane Sawyer, Robin Roberts, Chris Cuomo and Sam Champion do their thing, call 212–580–5176, or show up weekday mornings to Times Square at 44th Street and Broadway, from 7 A.M. to 9 A.M. to watch from the street.

More info is at abcnews.go.com/GMA/story.

Last Call with Carson Daly

Last Call with Carson Daly
330 Bob Hope Drive
Burbank, CA 91523

Call 1–888–4LC-TIXX or visit www.1lota.com for tickets. Stand-by tickets can be acquired at the NBC Experience Store at 49th Street and Rockefeller Plaza, but that will only get you in if there's room.

Late Night with Conan O'Brien

Send a postcard with your name, address, and phone number, including the number of tickets you want to:

Conan O'Brien
NBC Tickets
30 Rockefeller Plaza
New York, NY 10112

See what Conan's been up to at: www.nbc.com/Late_Night_with_Conan_O'Brien/index.shtml

Late Show with David Letterman

Send a postcard with your name, address, and phone number to:

David Letterman Tickets
Ed Sullivan Theater
1697 Broadway
New York, NY 10019

Generally it will take nine months or longer to receive an answer, so be prepared to wait. Alternatively, you can line up at 9:00 A.M. at the Ed Sullivan ticket office and hope for cancellations (of which there are many due to the long wait between booking and the show).

The show's Web site is at: www.cbs.com/latenight/lateshow/.

Live with Regis & Kelly

Write to:

Live Tickets
P.O. Box 230777
Ansonia Station
New York, NY 10023

You may have to wait a year or longer for reserved tickets to this show. Stand-by passes are given out beginning at 7:00 A.M. each day at their studio (corner of West 67th and Columbus Avenue).

You'll find the official show Web site at: www.bventertainment.go.com/tv/buenavista/regisandkelly/index.html

The Martha Stewart Show

The Martha Stewart Show
Chelsea Studios
221 West 26th Street
New York, NY 10001

For tickets to *The Martha Stewart Show*, visit the Web site below to submit your request: www.marthastewart.com/the-martha-stewart-show.

Rachael Ray

Fill out the online ticket request form at www.rachaelrayshow.com/show-info/audience-tickets/.

Tyra

Tyra Chelsea Studios
221 West 26th Street
New York, NY 10001

Call 1–888-SEE-TYRA or visit www.TyraShow.com

The Today Show

The Today Show
30 Rockefeller Plaza
New York, New York 10112

Show up early, before 7 A.M., to get a good spot at 49th Street and Rockefeller Plaza if you'd like to try to get on as background or as an interviewed fan of *The Today Show*. If you hang out around the southeast corner, you'll be behind where the anchors sit. It will probably help your chances to be on camera if you dress like a chicken, have a cute child in your arms, or construct a 12-foot sign that says "Kansas Loves Al!"

You can learn more about *The Today Show* at: www.msnbc.msn.com/id/3079108/.

The View

Write to:

The View Tickets
320 W. 66th Street
New York, NY 10023

Or visit www.abc.com/theview

Standby tickets are available from 10 A.M. each day on a first-come, first-served basis at ABC Studios at 320 W. 66th Street at West End Avenue.

Visit **Contact Any Celebrity** (www.ContactAnyCelebrity.com) to get the direct mailing addresses of over 41 radio and television talk show hosts.

chapter

SEVEN

Television Hosts & News Anchors

"There's a little more ego involved in these jobs than people might realize."

—WALTER CRONKITE

In addition to hosts of talk shows, other types of celebrities include hosts of a wide range of other types of TV programs as well as national and local news anchors. Sometimes we see these folks' faces so often, it feels like we already know them. Below are some ideas for how to make a connection with this type of celebrity.

Meeting in Person

One possible way to run into news anchors is by going on a tour of a network's studio. One of the most popular news network tours is the **CNN Studio Tour** in Atlanta.

CNN Studio Tour
190 Marietta Street
Atlanta, GA 30303
404-827-2300 (Phone)
www.cnn.com/studiotour

Sending Fan Mail

The best way to contact national program hosts and news anchors is through their network. Write to those folks at their respective network, but send mail to a local personality at your local channel (even if the station where they appear is a local affiliate of a national network). You can usually find the local addresses by doing a search on Google for something like "NBC affiliate Atlanta" as an example and then locating the station's address on their Web site.

Visit **Contact Any Celebrity** (www.ContactAnyCelebrity.com) to get the direct mailing addresses of over 231 television hosts and news anchors.

Major Television Network Addresses

A&E Television Networks
235 E. 45th Street
New York, NY 10017
212-210-1400 (Phone)
212-983-4370 (Fax)
www.aetv.com

ABC Entertainment Television Group (ABC)
500 S. Buena Vista Street
Burbank, CA 91521
818-460-7777 (Phone)
www.abc.com

AMC
200 Jericho Quadrangle
Jericho, NY 11753
516-803-3000 (Phone)
www.amctv.com

Animal Planet
One Discovery Place
Silver Spring, MD 20910
240-662-2000 (Phone)
240-662-1845 (Fax)
firstname_lastname@discovery.com
animal.discovery.com

BBC America
7475 Wisconsin Avenue
Bethesda, MD 20814
301-347-2222 (Phone)
301-656-8073 (Fax)
www.bbcamerica.com

Black Entertainment Television Network (BET-DC)
One BET Plaza
1235 W Street NE
Washington, DC 20018
202-608-2000 (Phone)
202-608-2631 (Fax)
www.bet.com

Black Entertainment Television Network (BET-LA)
4024 Radford Avenue
R&D Building, Floor 4
Studio City, CA 91604
818-655-6700 (Phone)
818-655-6770 (Fax)
www.bet.com

Bravo Network (LA)
3000 W. Alameda Avenue
Burbank, CA 91523
818-840-4444
www.bravotv.com

Bravo Network (NY)
30 Rockefeller Plaza, #14-E
New York, NY 10112
212-664-4444 (Phone)
www.bravotv.com

British Broadcasting Company (BBC)
Wood Lane
London W12 8QC
UNITED KINGDOM
011-44-20-8433-2000
bbc.co.uk

Cable News Network (CNN)
Turner Broadcasting Systems
One CNN Center
P.O. Box 105366
Atlanta, GA 30348
404-827-1500
firstname.lastname@turner.com
www.cnn.com

Cartoon Network
1050 Techwood Drive NW
Atlanta, GA 30318
404-885-2263 (Phone)
404-885-4312 (Fax)
www.cartoonnetwork.com

CBS Entertainment (LA)
7800 Beverly Boulevard
Los Angeles, CA 90036
323-575-2345 (Phone)
www.cbs.com

CBS Entertainment (NY)
51 W. 52nd Street, Floor 6
New York, NY 10019
212-975-4321 (Phone)
www.cbs.com

The Christian Broadcasting Network (TBN)
977 Centerville Turnpike
Virginia Beach, VA 23463
757-226-7000 (Phone)
www.cbn.com

Cinemax
1100 Ave. of the Americas
New York, NY 10036
212-512-1000 (Phone)
www.cinemax.com

CMT: Country Music Television (LA)
2600 Colorado Avenue
Santa Monica, CA 90404
310-752-8248 (Phone)
www.cmt.com

CMT: Country Music Television (TN)
3300 Commerce Street
Nashville, TN 37201
615-335-8400 (Phone)
615-335-8619 (Fax)
www.cmt.com

CNBC
900 Sylvan Avenue
Englewood Cliff, NJ 07632
201-735-2622 (Phone)
201-735-3200 (Fax)
www.cnbc.com

Comedy Central (LA)
2049 Century Park East, #4170
Los Angeles, CA 90067
310-407-4700 (Phone)
310-407-4797 (Fax)
www.comedycentral.com

Comedy Central (NY)
1775 Broadway, Floor 10
New York, NY 10019
212-767-8600 (Phone)
212-767-8592 (Fax)
www.comedycentral.com

Court TV
600 Third Avenue
New York, NY 10016
212-973-2800 (Phone)
212-973-3210 (Fax)
www.courttv.com

Discovery Networks
One Discovery Place
Silver Spring, MD 20910
240-662-2000 (Phone)
240-662-1845 (Fax)
firstname_lastname@discovery.com
www.discovery.com

Disney Channel
3800 W. Alameda Avenue
Burbank, CA 91505
818-569-7500
www.disneychannel.com

E! Networks
5750 Wilshire Blvd.
Los Angeles, CA 90036
323-954-2400 (Phone)
323-954-2662 (Fax)
www.eonline.com

ESPN (CT)
ESPN Plaza
Bristol, CT 06010
860-766-2000 (Phone)
www.espn.com

ESPN (NY)
605 Third Avenue, Floor 8
New York, NY 10158
212-916-9200 (Phone)
www.espn.com

Food Network
1180 Avenue of the Americas
New York, NY 10036
212-398-8836 (Phone)
212-997-0997 (Fax)
www.foodnetwork.com

Fox Broadcasting Company
P.O. Box 900
Beverly Hills, CA 90213
310-369-1000 (Phone)
www.fox.com

Fox News Channel
1440 S. Sepulveda Boulevard
Los Angeles, CA 90025
310-444-8752 (Phone)
310-444-8665 (Fax)
www.foxnews.com

Fox Sports Network
10201 W. Pico Boulevard
Building 101
Los Angeles, CA 90035
310-369-1000 (Phone)
www.foxsports.com

FX
2121 Avenue of the Stars, Floor 19
Los Angeles, CA 90067
310-369-1000 (Phone)
310-969-4688 (Fax)
www.fxnetworks.com

Game Show Network
10202 Washington Boulevard
Culver City, CA 90232
310-244-222
www.gsn.com

HBO Enterprises (LA)
1100 Avenue of the Americas
New York, NY 10036
212-512-1000 (Phone)
212-512-5698 (Fax)
www.hbo.com

HBO, Inc.
2500 Broadway, #400
Santa Monica, CA 90404
310-382-3000 (Phone)
www.hbo.com

Home & Garden Television (HGTV)
9721 Sherrill Boulevard
Knoxville, TN 37932
865-694-2700 (Phone)
865-531-1588 (Fax)
www.hgtv.com

Home Shopping Network
1 HSN Drive
St. Petersburg, FL 33729
727-872-1000 (Phone)
www.hsn.com

The Independent Film Channel (IFC)
200 Jericho Quadrangle
Jericho, NY 11753
516-803-4500 (Phone)
516-803-4506 (Fax)
www.ifctv.com

Lifetime Television (LA)
2049 Century Park East, #840
Los Angeles, CA 90067
310-556-7500 (Phone)
www.lifetimetv.com

Lifetime Television (NY)
309 W. 49th Street, Floor 16
New York, NY 10019
212-424-7000 (Phone)
212-957-4264 (Fax)
www.lifetimetv.com

LOGO
1775 Broadway, Floor 11
New York, NY 10019
212-258-8000 (Phone)
212-767-4460 (Fax)
www.logo-tv.com

MSNBC
One MSNBC Plaza
Secaucus, NJ 07094
201-583-5000 (Phone)
viewerservices@msnbc.com
www.msnbc.com

MTV Networks (LA)
2600 Colorado Avenue
Santa Monica, CA 90404
310-752-8000 (Phone)
www.mtv.com

MTV Networks (NY)
1515 Broadway
New York, NY 10036
212-258-8000 (Phone)
www.mtv.com

National Broadcasting Network (NBC)
3000 W. Alameda Avenue, #5366
Burbank, CA 91523
818-840-3532 (Phone)
www.nbc.com

Nickelodeon (LA)
2600 Colorado Avenue
Santa Monica, CA 90404
310-752-8000 (Phone)
www.nick.com

Nickelodeon (NY)
1515 Broadway, Floor 38
New York, NY 10036
212-258-7500 (Phone)
www.nick.com

PAX
601 Clearwater Park Road
West Palm Beach, FL 33401
561-659-4122 (Phone)
561-682-4236 (Fax)
www.pax.tv

PBS
1320 Braddock Place
Alexandria, VA 22314
703-739-5000 (Phone)
703-739-0775 (Fax)
www.pbs.org

Playboy Entertainment Group
2706 Media Center Drive
Los Angeles, CA 90065
323-276-4000 (Phone)
323-276-4500 (Fax)
www.plaboytv.com

Quality Value Convenience (QVC)
1200 Wilson Drive
West Chester, PA 19380
1-800-200-0777 (Phone)
www.qvc.com

Sci-Fi Channel (LA)
100 Universal City Plaza
Building 1440, Floor 14
Universal City, CA 91608
818-777-1000 (Phone)
www.scifi.com

Sci-Fi Channel (NY)
1230 Avenue of the Americas
New York, NY 10020
212-664-4444 (Phone)
212-703-8533 (Fax)
www.scifi.com

Showtime Networks, Inc. (LA)
10880 Wilshire Boulevard, #1600
Los Angeles, CA 90024
310-234-5200 (Phone)
www.sho.com

Showtime Networks, Inc. (NY)
1633 Broadway
New York, NY 10019
212-708-1600 (Phone)
www.sho.com

SOAPNET
3800 W. Alameda Avenue
Burbank, CA 91505
818-569-7500 (Phone)
818-566-7402 (Fax)
www.soapnet.com

Spike TV
1515 Broadway
New York, NY 10036
212-258-8000 (Phone)
www.spiketv.com

Starz Entertainment
8900 Liberty Circle
Englewood, CO 80112
720-852-7700 (Phone)
720-852-7760 (Fax)
www.starz.com

TBS (ATL)
1050 Techwood Drive NW
Atlanta, GA 30318
404-827-1700 (Phone)
404-885-4673 (Fax)
firstname.lastname@turner.com
www.tbs.com

TBS (LA)
3500 W. Olive Avenue, Floor 15
Burbank, CA 91505
818-977-5500 (Phone)
firstname.lastname@turner.com
www.tbs.com

Telemundo
2290 W. Eighth Avenue
Hialeah, FL 33010
305-884-8200 (Phone)
www.telemundo.com

TLC
One Discovery Place
Silver Spring, MD 20910
240-662-2000 (Phone)
240-662-1845 (Fax)
tlc.discovery.com

Travel Channel
One Discovery Place
Silver Spring, MD 20910
240-662-2000 (Phone)
240-662-1845 (Fax)
travel.discovery.com

Trinity Broadcasting Network (TBN)
2823 W. Irving Boulevard
Irving, TX 75061
1-800-735-5542 (Phone)
www.tbn.org

Turner Network Television (TNT)
1050 Techwood Drive
Atlanta, GA 30318
404-827-1500 (Phone)
404-885-4947 (Fax)
firstname.lastname@turner.com
www.tnt.tv

Univision 34
5999 Center Drive
Los Angeles, CA 90045
310-216-3434 (Phone)
www.univision.com

UPN
1800 Wilshire Boulevard
Los Angeles, CA 90025
310-575-7000 (Phone)
www.upn.com

USA Network (LA)
100 Universal City Plaza
Universal City, CA 91608
818-777-1000 (Phone)
www.usanetwork.com

USA Network (NY)
30 Rockefeller Plaza, Floor 21
New York, NY 10112
212-664-4444 (Phone)
www.usanetwork.com

VH1 (LA)
2600 Colorado Avenue
Santa Monica, CA 90404
310-752-8000
www.vh1.com

VH1 (NY)
1515 Broadway
New York, NY 10036
212-846-8000 (Phone)
www.vh1.com

Video Hits One (VH1)
2600 Colorado Avenue
Santa Monica, CA 90404
310-752-8000
www.vh1.com

The WB Television Network (LA)
4000 Warner Boulevard
Building 34R
Burbank, CA 91522
818-977-5000 (Phone)
818-977-2282 (Fax)
thewb.warnerbros.com

The WB Television Network (NY)
1325 Avenue of the Americas
New York, NY 10019
212-636-5049 (Phone)
www.thewb.com

WE: Women's Nework
200 Jericho Quadrangle
Jericho, NY 11753
516-803-3000 (Phone)
www.we.tv

The Weather Channel
Landmark Networks
300 Interstate North Parkway
Atlanta, GA 30339
770-226-0000 (Phone)
www.weather.com

chapter
EIGHT

Baseball Players

*"Baseball fans love numbers. They love to swirl
them around their mouths like Bordeaux wine."*

—PAT CONROY

Getting in touch with a professional baseball player for an autograph or piece of memorabilia used to be really easy. You simply lined up outside the locker room after the game and talked to the players as they left for their cars. Or maybe you leaned over the outfield wall and convinced a player to come over and sign something as he retrieved a foul ball. Or perhaps you even dropped a pen and a baseball into the bullpen and waited for it to get thrown back up to you.

But that's not so true anymore.

Jose Canseco began to move away from providing free autographs for fans when he started charging kids five bucks per signature at Major League Baseball games. At the time, this was considered heresy, but Canseco was actually ahead of the curve. What started out as a nice gesture between player and fan soon became an industry. The player quite rightfully feels used when he takes time out of his schedule to do a kid a favor and that kid turns around and sells his autograph to a memorabilia vendor for $10.

How to "Catch" a Player's Signature

There are four main ways to get a baseball player to sign for you:

1. An open autograph period. Most teams have times when players are permitted to sign things for the fans—usually around batting practice time, after a big win, or at an official team event. If you go to the ballpark four hours before game time, you'll see the players having an early swing in a low-pressure environment. While they're waiting their turn, you're generally not scowled at too much if you approach them with a handshake and a pen.

2. A charity event. Nearly every Major League Baseball player—as well as those in the Major Leagues—is aligned with various charities where he turns up to assist a few times per year. In fact, many players have charitable foundations of their own that they've set up to help a certain cause. Since the player gives his time to the cause at these charity events, it's expected that fans will be able to talk to him, approach him for signings, and just hang out. Your side of the bargain is to give a little to the charity in thanks—it's a fair trade.

3. Write to the player's team or club. This is a pretty easy option. Just send a letter to your favorite player through his team and ask if he wouldn't mind signing a photo or something else for you (or for your grandmother, child, or dog). Usually the player will oblige, especially if you're smart and put a self-addressed stamped envelope in the package so they don't have to pay return postage.

4. Get 'em early. Every ballplayer starts somewhere, and that somewhere is usually in a tiny ballpark in a tiny town where a tiny crowd turns up to see newcomers play. Nearly every region of North America has a minor league club somewhere nearby, and even independent league clubs can be a great place to get up-and-coming players as well as former big names now considering retirement. Most minor league teams will let fans come onto the field after a game to meet the players, especially after a win. But if they lose, don't expect them to stick around too long!

Former baseball player Sean Casey, always enjoyed signing autographs. "Some guys don't want to be bothered with it," he told the Cincinnati Enquirer in 2003. "That's fine. The bottom line is, it might put a smile on somebody's face. That's the point; it makes somebody happy."

Casey continued, "I get stories back from people about how I took two seconds out of my day to sign an autograph and it makes their day. It's neat to know you can have that kind of impact. I don't mind at all if people ask me, because I've done the same thing."

A case in point, Casey once showed up to a celebrity softball game with a bat, ball, and trading cards for Pete Rose to sign. "Pete Rose made me a little nervous. You get the big-time, Hall of Fame-type guys. They make you nervous until you find out they're good guys. I acted like a little kid."

Sometimes getting a player to agree to sign something takes a little psychology as well as patience. Especially in the minor leagues, these guys are playing for their futures with every swing of the bat, so taking a flash photo of them when they are cocked and ready to swing as a pitch is thrown their way isn't likely to endear you to them. Neither will sticking your head over the top of the dugout, or getting annoyed if a player refuses your request to interrupt his schedule for a signature.

But you can change the odds in your favor. If you bring a player's baseball card to the park and ask him to sign it, he's likely to be impressed that it was him you wanted to see. If you buy a ball from the souvenir stand, likewise they're more likely to sign it since you're helping the team. If you catch a pop foul and present the ball to the player who hit it after the game, he'll appreciate the value of signing the ball and will likely do just that. Alternately, if you're waiting at the stadium gate with 12 baseballs to sign, you're going to be pegged as someone just looking to make a little cash on the player's time.

Remember that today's minor league star could be tomorrow's starting pitcher for the Boston Red Sox, and minor league memorabilia surrounding his early career is not only more unique than a signed baseball card, it can also become valuable when that red-faced kid from Round Rock, Texas, becomes the next baseball All Star player. At about six bucks a ticket for a minor league game, there's really not a huge expense involved in staking out the local ballpark and looking for the next big thing.

Sending Fan Mail to a Baseball Player

To write to your favorite baseball player, send your letter to the player's respective team.

Visit **Contact Any Celebrity** (www.ContactAnyCelebrity.com) to get the direct mailing addresses for over 6,633 professional baseball players.

Major League Baseball Team Addresses

Los Angeles Angels of Anaheim
2000 Gene Autry Way
Anaheim, CA 92806
1-888-796-HALO (4256)
www.LAAngels.com

Arizona Diamondbacks
P.O. Box 2095
Phoenix, AZ 85001
602-462-6500
www.ArizondDiamondbacks.com

Atlanta Braves
P.O. Box 4064
Atlanta, GA 30302
404-522-7630
www.AtlantaBraves.com

Baltimore Orioles
Oriole Park at Camden Yards
333 W. Camden Street
Baltimore, MD 21201
410-685-9800
www.TheOrioles.com

Boston Red Sox
4 Yawkey Way
Boston, MA 02215
617-267-9440
www.RedSox.com

Chicago Cubs
Wrigley Field
1060 West Addison
Chicago, IL 60613
773-404-CUBS (2827)
www.cubs.com

Chicago White Sox
333 W. 35th Street
Chicago, IL 60616
312-674-1000
www.WhiteSox.com

Cincinnati Reds
100 Main Street
Cincinnati, OH 45202
513-765-7000
www.CincinnatiReds.com

Cleveland Indians
Jacobs Field
2401 Ontario Street
Cleveland, OH 44155
216-420-4636
www.Indians.com

Colorado Rockies
Coors Field
2001 Blake Street
Denver, CO 80205
303-ROCKIES (762-5437)
www.ColoradoRockies.com

Detroit Tigers
Comercia Park
2100 Woodward Avenue
Detroit, MI 48201
www.DetroitTigers.com

Florida Marlins
Dolphin Stadium
2269 Dan Marino Boulevard
Miami, FL 33056
305-626-7400
www.FLAMarlins.com

Houston Astros
P.O. Box 288
Houston, TX 77001
713-259-8000
www.Astros.com

Kansas City Royals
One Royal Way
Kansas City, MO 64129
816-921-8000
www.Royals.com

Los Angeles Dodgers
Dodger Stadium
1000 Elysian Park Avenue
Los Angeles, CA 90012
323-225-6514
www.LADodgers.com

Milwaukee Brewers
1 Brewers Way
Milwaukee, WI 53214
414-902-4400
www.MilwaukeeBrewers.com

Minnesota Twins
Metrodome
34 Kirby Puckett Place
Minneapolis, MN 55415
612-375-1366
www.MinnesotaTwins.com

New York Yankees
161st Street & River Avenue
Bronx, NY 10452
718-293-4300
www.Yankees.com

Oakland Athletics
Oakland Coliseum
7000 Coliseum Way
Oakland, CA 94621
510-638-4900
www.OaklandAthletics.com

Philadelphia Phillies
One Citizens Bank Way
Citizens Bank Ballpark
Philadelphia, PA 19148
215-463-6000
www.Phillies.com

Pittsburgh Pirates
PNC Park at North Shore
115 Federal Street
Pittsburgh, PA 15212
412-323-5000
www.PittsburghPirates.com

St. Louis Cardinals
Busch Stadium
700 Clark Street
St. Louis, MO 63102
314-345-9600
www.StLCardinals.com

San Diego Padres
P.O. Box 2000
San Diego, CA 92112
619-735-5000
www.Padres.com

San Francisco Giants
SBC Park
24 Willie Mays Plaza
San Francisco, CA 94107
415-972-2000
www.SFGiants.com

Seattle Mariners
P.O. Box 4100
411 First Avenue South
Seattle, WA 98194
206-346-4000
www.SeattleMariners.com

Tampa Bay Rays
Tropicana Field
One Tropicana Drive
St. Petersburg, FL 33705
727-825-3137
www.RaysBaseball.com

Texas Rangers
1000 Ballpark Way
Arlington, TX 76011
817-273-5222
www.TexasRangers.com

Toronto Blue Jays
1 Blue Jays Way, #3200
Rogers Centre
Toronto, ON M5V 1J1
CANADA
416-341-1000
www.BlueJays.com

Washington Nationals
Nationals Park
1500 South Capitol Street, SE
Washington, D.C. 20003-1507
202-349-0400
www.Nationals.com

Triple-A Baseball League Addresses

International League
55 South High Street, #202
Dublin, OH 43017
614-791-9300
www.ILBaseball.com

Pacific Coast League
1631 Mesa Avenue, #A
Colorado Springs, CO 80906
719-636-3399
www.PCLBaseball.com

Double-A Baseball League Addresses

Eastern League
30 Danforth Street, #208
Portland, ME 04101
207-761-2700
www.EasternLeague.com

Texas League
2442 Facet Oak
San Antonio, TX 78232
210-545-5297
www.Texas-League.com

Southern League
2551 Roswell Road, #330
Marietta, GA 30062
770-321-0400
www.SouthernLeague.com

Class-A Baseball League Addresses

California League
2380 South Bascom Avenue, #200
Campbell, CA 95008
408-369-8038
www.CaliforniaLeague.com

Carolina League
P.O. Box 9503
Greensboro, NC 27429
336-691-9030
www.CarolinaLeague.com

Florida State League
P.O. Box 349
Daytona Beach, FL 32115
386-252-7479
www.FSLBaseball.com

Midwest League
P.O. Box 936
Beloit, WI 53512
608-364-1188
www.MidwestLeague.com

Northwest League
P.O. Box 1645
Boise, ID 83701
208-429-1511
www.NorthwestLeague.com

South Atlantic League
504 Crescent Hill Road
Kings Mountain, NC 28086
704-739-3466
www.SouthAtlanticLeague.com

Rookie Baseball League Addresses

Appalachian League
283 Deerchase Circle
Statesville, NC 28625
704-873-5300
www.AppyLeague.com

Arizona League
P.O. Box 1645
Boise, ID 83701
208-429-1511

Gulf Coast League
1503 Clover Creek Drive, #H262
Sarasota, FL 34231
941-966-6407

Pioneer League
P.O. Box 2564
Spokane, WA 99220
509-456-7615
www.PioneerLeague.com

Spring Training

Spring Training is a great time to find a large number of Major League (and Minor League) players in one place. Every year around February, all the Major League franchises start their preparations for the coming baseball season by flying down to Florida or Arizona. Once there, the baseball players take part in scratch games against other teams and even their own teammates.

With the pressure of the regular season not yet upon them, many players are far more agreeable to signing things, shaking hands, and having their picture taken by fans. If you decide to take an early spring vacation to the world of Spring Training, visit my Web site Contact Any Celebrity at www.contactanycelebrity.com/spring-training/ first to obtain a list of places you can stake out.

Arizona Spring Training

Los Angeles Angels of Anaheim
Tempe Diablo Stadium
2200 W. Alameda Drive
Tempe, AZ 85282

Arizona Diamondbacks
Tucson Electric Park
2500 E. Ajo Way
Tucson, AZ 85713

Chicago Cubs
HoHoKam Park
1235 N. Center Street
Mesa, AZ 85201

Chicago White Sox
Tucson Electric Park
2500 E. Ajo Way
Tucson, AZ 85713

Colorado Rockies
Hi Corbett Field
3400 E. Camino Camestre
Tucson, AZ 85713

Milwaukee Brewers
Maryvale Baseball Park
3805 W. 53rd Avenue
Phoenix, AZ 85031

Oakland Athletics
Phoenix Municipal Stadium
5999 E. Van Buren
Phoenix, AZ 85008

San Diego Padres
Peoria Sports Complex
16101 N. 83rd Avenue
Peoria, AZ 85382

San Francisco Giants
Scottsdale Stadium
7408 E. Osborn Road
Scottsdale, AZ 85251

Florida Spring Training

Atlanta Braves
Disney Wide World of Sports Stadium
700 S. Victory Way
Kissimmee, FL 34747

Baltimore Orioles
Ft. Lauderdale Stadium
5301 N.W. 12th Avenue
Ft. Lauderdale, FL 33309

Boston Red Sox
City of Palms Park
2201 Edison Avenue
Fort Meyers, FL 33901

Cincinnati Reds
Ed Smith Stadium
2700 12th Street
Sarasota, FL 34237

Cleveland Indians
Chain of Lakes Park
Cypress Gardens Blvd.
Winter Haven, FL 33880

Detroit Tigers
Tiger Town
P.O. Box 90187
Lakeland, FL 33804

Florida Marlins
Space Coast Stadium
5800 Stadium Parkway
Melbourne, FL 32940

Houston Astros
Osceola Country Stadium
1000 Bill Beck Boulevard
Kissimmee, FL 34744

Kansas City Royals
Baseball City Stadium
300 Stadium Way
Davenport, FL 33837

Los Angeles Dodgers
Holman Stadium
4101 26th Street
Vero Beach, FL 32961

Minnesota Twins
Hammond Stadium
14100 Six Mile Cypress Parkway
Ft. Meyers, FL 33912

Montreal Expos
Roger Dean Stadium
P.O. Box 8976
Jupiter, FL 3348

New York Mets
St. Lucie Sports Complex
525 N.W. Peacock Boulevard
Port St. Lucie, FL 34986

Philadelphia Phillies
Jack Russell Stadium
800 Phillies Drive
Clearwater, FL 34615

Pittsburgh Pirates
McKechnie Field
17th Avenue & 9th Street W.
Bradenton, FL 34208

Seattle Mariners
Peoria Sports Complex
15707 N 83rd Avenue
Ft. Meyers, FL 33901

St. Louis Cardinals
Roger Dean Stadium
4751 Main Street
Jupiter, FL 33458

Tampa Bay Devil Rays
Florida Power Park
180 Second Avenue S.E.
St. Petersburg, FL 33701

Texas Rangers
Charlotte County Stadium
2300 El Jobean Road
Port Charlotte, FL 33948

Toronto Blue Jays
Dunedin Stadium at Grant Field
311 Douglas Avenue
Dunedin, FL 34696

chapter

NINE

Football Players

*"The difference between a successful person
and others is not a lack of strength, not a
lack of knowledge, but a lack of will."*

—VINCE LOMBARDI

When New England Patriots quarterback Tom Brady was eight years old, he found himself in the San Francisco Giants' locker room. While there, he asked Chili Davis, a star for the team at the time, for an autograph. Davis refused, but said, "Maybe later kid, maybe if you come by after the game." So the young Brady stuck around the stadium, and after the game, he re-approached his favorite player, only to be turned away again. Davis told him: "No, I'm not signing autographs after the game."

Later, in an interview with *Tuff Stuff* magazine, Brady reflected on the incident. "I certainly was hurt," he said, "but at the same time, I was in the guy's clubhouse and now I look at it from a different perspective than I did when I was that age. At the time, though, it seemed like such a little request."

One would expect that walking into the Patriots' locker room and asking for autographs might be a fast way to get your butt kicked. Still, there are ways you can stray into the autograph-giver's radar without becoming a nuisance.

1. You must have something to sign. Having a player sign your arm may seem like a fun idea at the time—and they may well oblige—but it's largely a pointless act since you're going to eventually wash it off. A good rule of thumb is if you're not going straight to the tattoo parlor to have a tattoo artist trace the autograph, don't bother with body-signing.

2. Always carry a good quality pen. What's the point of handing the player something to sign if you don't have something to sign it with?

3. Know who you're talking to when you ask for the autograph. If you can call the player by name, or say something that shows you have taken an interest in him, he's going to look at you more positively than someone else.

4. Remember that the real estate mantra "location, location, location" also applies here. It's far easier to get a player to sign something from front row seats than from seats in the second balcony!

If you get tickets for a good seat and arrive at the game early, you can also talk to the players as they walk by. Once you get one in conversation, you might end up having a few other players stop by as well. Sometimes a player will start signing autographs and a crowd will quickly form, which is another reason to get to the game early. Fighting a crowd for signatures—or worse, being in your seat as dozens of fans start crowding around you—is likely to get annoying.

If you can learn where the players come in and out of the stadium, that's another great place to find them, ask for signatures, pose for photos, shake hands, etc. The baseball players are far more likely to stick around for a while when not in a hurry.

Sending Fan Mail to a NFL Player

Whenever you're just looking for a signed photo, you can write the player care of his team's address. A better way is to also include an unsigned 8x10 photo along with a self-addressed stamped envelope.

Visit **Contact Any Celebrity** (www.contactanycelebrity.com) to get the direct mailing addresses for over 8,069 professional football players.

NFL Team Addresses

Arizona Cardinals
P.O. Box 888
Phoenix, AZ 85001
602-379-0101
www.AZCardinals.com

Atlanta Falcons
4400 Falcon Parkway
Flowery Branch, GA 30542
770-965-3115
www.AtlantaFalcons.com

Baltimore Ravens
M&T Bank Stadium
1101 Russell Street
Baltimore, MD 21230
410-547-8100
www.BaltimoreRavens.com

Buffalo Bills
One Bills Drive
Orchard Park, NY 14127
716-646-9229
www.BuffaloBills.com

Carolina Panthers
800 S. Mint Street
Charlotte, NC 28202
704-358-7000
www.Panthers.com

Chicago Bears
Halas Hall
1000 Football Drive
Lake Forest, IL 60045
847-295-6600
www.ChicagoBears.com

Cincinnati Bengals
One Paul Brown Stadium
Cincinnati, OH 45202
513-621-3550
www.Bengals.com

Cleveland Browns
Cleveland Brows Stadium
100 Alfred Lerner Way
Cleveland, OH 44114
440-891-5000
www.ClevelandBrowns.com

Dallas Cowboys
Cowboys Center
One Cowboys Parkway
Irving, TX 75063
972-910-0797
www.DallasCowboys.com

Denver Broncos
13655 Broncos Parkway
Englewood, CO 80112
303-649-9000
www.DenverBroncos.com

Detroit Lions
222 Republic Drive
Allen Park, MI 48101
313-216-4056
www.DetroitLions.com

Green Bay Packers
P.O. Box 10628
Green Bay, WI 54307
920-569-7500
www.Packers.com

Houston Texans
Two Reliant Park
Houston, TX 77054
832-667-2000
www.HoustonTexans.com

Indianapolis Colts
7001 West 56th Street
Indianapolis, IN 46254
1-800-805-258
www.Colts.com

Jacksonville Jaguars
One Alltel Stadium Place
Jacksonville, FL 32202
1-800-618-8005
www.Jaguars.com

Kansas City Chiefs
One Arrowhead Drive
Kansas City, MO 64129
816-920-9300
www.KCChiefs.com

Miami Dolphins
7500 SW 30th Street
Davie, FL 33314
954-452-7000
www.MiamiDolphins.com

Minnesota Vikings
9520 Viking Drive
Eden Prairie, MN 55344
952-828-500
www.Vikings.com

New England Patriots
One Patriot Place
Foxboro, MA 02035
508-543-8200
www.Patriots.com

New Orleans Saints
5800 Airline Drive
Metairie, LA 70003
504-731-1862
www.NewOrleansSaints.com

New York Giants
Giants Stadium
East Rutherford, NJ 07073
201-935-8111
www.Giants.com

New York Jets
1000 Fulton Avenue
Hempstead, NY 11550
516-538-6601
www.NewYorkJets.com

Oakland Raiders
1220 Harbor Bay Parkway
Alameda, CA 94502
510-864-5000
www.Raiders.com

Philadelphia Eagles
One Novacare Way
Philadelphia, PA 19145
215-463-2500
www.PhiladelphiaEagles.com

Pittsburgh Steelers
P.O. Box 6763
Pittsburgh, PA 15212
412-432-7800
www.Steelers.com

San Diego Chargers
P.O. Box 609609
San Diego, CA 92160-9609
858-874-4500
www.Chargers.com

San Francisco 49ers
4949 Centennial Boulevard
Santa Clara, CA 95054
408-562-4949
www.SF49ers.com

Seattle Seahawks
11220 N.E. 53rd Street
Kirkland, WA 98033
425-827-9777
www.Seahawks.com

St. Louis Rams
One Rams Way
St. Louis, MO 63045
314-982-7267
www.StLouisRams.com

Tampa Bay Buccaneers
One Buccaneer Place
Tampa, FL 33607
813-870-2700
www.Buccaneers.com

Tennessee Titans
One Titans Way
Nashville, TN 37213
615-565-4200
www.TitansOnline.com

Washington Redskins
21300 Redskin Park
Ashburn, VA 22011
www.RedSkins.com

chapter
TEN

Basketball Players

*"If all I'm remembered for is being good
as a basketball player, then I've done a
bad job with the rest of my life."*

—ISIAH THOMAS

Getting an autograph from a National Basketball Association (NBA) player is a tall order—in more ways than just their sometimes incredible height! NBA sports stars make a lot of money, play in big stadiums with a limited number of front row seats, and train in facilities that are usually not open to the public. That's not to say, however, that you won't find a willing signer at an NBA game who will adorn your items with his John Hancock. You just have to work a little harder than with some other sports.

Front row seats at an NBA game are the best way to get the attention of a player. They probably won't give you any time during a game, since doing so would bring a beat down from the coaching staff. However, between quarters, before the game, and after the final buzzer, front row seats are a goldmine.

Also, basketball players, like people involved in many other sports, usually will warm up more toward children. Amare Stoudemire, a six foot,

10 inch Rookie of the Year, has offered some insight into this. "Some adults, all they want to do is put the autograph on eBay and sell it. I'm not a fan of that. I just don't like it when they make money off my autographs. I want to give out autographs for them to keep if I'm their favorite player or whatnot. Kids, they're going to cherish the autograph and that's going to show they have a certain amount of love in their heart. When I was a kid, I always wanted to get a professional player's autograph, so I try to give most of my time off the court to the kids, because that's the future." On eBay, by the way, Stoudemire's autographs can go for as much as $80 a piece.

If you don't have a kid brother to bring to the game, a good way to meet the players is to arrive early and try to find them wandering around courtside before their pre-game warm-up. An investment in a seat located close to the court will be helpful in this approach because ushers aren't likely to let someone sitting in the nosebleeds get down to the bench. Depending, however, on how early you arrive, it's very possible to find players in a talkative mood before the crowds descend on the place.

Perhaps a better spot to find players who will sign something is to get them while they're in college, or playing in other leagues that are found in North America like the CBA (Continental Basketball Association). College basketball is huge, but not so big that you can't find a side door to the stadium where the players will eventually come out or a local bar where they kick back after a win.

Another option is to contact the team and ask when the players are available for autographs. Many teams have a time of day or week when they actually encourage their players to meet the fans, and sometimes the sessions are sponsored by companies that pay the players for their time. Although attendance at these events can get you a lot of autographs in one hit, it can also mean a lot of standing around and waiting for the other thousand folks in line to have their turn.

One recent change in basketball autograph hunting has been the rise to fame of high school basketball. Players like the New Orleans Hornets' seven-foot, one-inch Tyson Chandler didn't merely come to the NBA straight out of high school. They were being scouted and talked about three years before, giving you as a fan a lot of time to find that kid, tell him what a great player he is, and get him to pose for a snapshot. Then get ready for that snapshot to be worth a whole lot of money a few years down the road when he signs his first multi-million dollar Nike deal.

Sending Fan Mail to NBA Players

To write to your favorite basketball player, simply send your letter to the office for their respective team.

Visit **Contact Any Celebrity** (www.ContactAnyCelebrity.com) to get the direct mailing addresses for over 1,370 professional basketball players.

NBA Basketball Team Addresses

Atlanta Hawks
Centennial Tower
101 Marietta St., #1900
Atlanta, GA 30303
404-878-3800
www.nba.com/hawks

Boston Celtics
226 Causeway St., Floor 4
Boston, MA 02114
917-854-8000
www.nba.com/celtics

Chicago Bulls
United Center
1901 West Madison Street
Chicago, IL 60612
312-455-4000
www.nba.com/bulls

Cleveland Cavaliers
One Center Court
Cleveland, OH 44115
216-420-2000
www.nba.com/cavaliers

Dallas Mavericks
The Pavilion
2909 Taylor Street
Dallas, TX 75226
274-747-MAVS (6287)
www.nba.com/mavericks

Denver Nuggets
Pepsi Center
1000 Chopper Circle
Denver, CO 80204
303-405-1100
www.nba.com/nuggets

Detroit Pistons
Palace of Auburn Hills
2 Championship Drive
Auburn Hills, MI 48326
248-377-0100
www.nba.com/pistons

Golden State Warriors
1011 Broadway, Floor 20
Oakland, CA 94607
510-986-2200
www.nba.com/warriors

Houston Rockets
1510 Polk Street
Houston, TX 77002
713-627-3865
www.nba.com/rockets

Indiana Pacers
125 S. Pennsylvania Street
Indianapolis, IN 46204
317-917-2500
www.nba.com/pacers

Los Angeles Clippers
Staples Center
111 S. Figueroa Street, #1100
Los Angeles, CA 90015
213-742-7500
www.nba.com/clippers

Los Angeles Lakers
555 N. Nash Street
El Segundo, CA 90245
310-426-6000
www.nba.com/lakers

Memphis Grizzlies
191 Beale Street
Memphis, TN 38103
901-205-1234
www.nba.com/grizzlies

Miami Heat
American Airlines Arena
601 Biscayne Boulevard
Miami, FL 33132
786-777-1000
www.nba.com/heat

Milwaukee Bucks
1001 N. Fourth St.
Milwaukee, WI 53203
414-227-0500
www.nba.com/bucks

Minnesota Timberwolves
600 First Ave. N.
Minneapolis, MN 55403
612-673-1600
www.nba.com/timberwolves

New Jersey Nets
Nets Champion Center
390 Murray Hill Parkway
East Rutherford, NJ 07073
1-800-7NJ-JETS (765-5387)
www.nba.com/nets

New Orleans Hornets
1501 Girod Street
New Orleans, LA 70113
504-301-4000
www.nba.com/hornets

New York Knicks
Madison Square Garden
2 Pennsylvania Plaza
New York, NY 10121
212-465-6471
www.nba.com/knicks

Orlando Magic
P.O. Box 76
Orlando, FL 32802
407-916-2400
www.nba.com/magic

Philadelphia 76ers
First Union Center
3601 S. Broad Street
Philadelphia, PA 19148
215-339-7600
www.nba.com/sixers

Phoenix Suns
201 E. Jefferson Street
Phoenix, AZ 85004
602-379-7900
www.nba.com/suns

Portland Trailblazers
One Center Court, #200
Portland, OR 97227
503-234-9291
www.nba.com/blazers

Sacramento Kings
One Sports Parkway
Sacramento, CA 95834
916-928-0000
www.nba.com/kings

San Antonio Spurs
One SBC Center
San Antonio, TX 78219
210-444-5000
www.nba.com/spurs

Seattle Supersonics
351 Elliot Avenue, West #500
Seattle, WA 98119
206-281-5800
www.nba.com/sonics

Toronto Raptors
Maple Leaf Sports
40 Bay Street, #400
Toronto, ON M5J 2X2
CANADA
416-815-5500
www.nba.com/raptors

Washington Wizards
MCI Center
601 F Street, NW
Washington, DC 20004
202-661-5100
www.nba.com/wizards

Utah Jazz
Delta Center
301 W. South Temple
Salt Lake City, UT 84101
801-325-2500
www.nba.com/jazz

WNBA Basketball Team Addresses

Charlotte Sting
129 W. Trade Street, #700
Charlotte, NC 28202
704-357-0252
www.wnba.com/sting

Connecticut Sun
One Mohegan Sun Boulevard
Uncasville, CT 06382
www.wnba.com/sun

Detroit Shock
Palace of Auburn Hills
4 Championship Drive
Auburn Hills, MI 48326
248-377-0100
www.wnba.com/shock

Houston Comets
1510 Polk Street
Houston, TX 77002
713-627-3865
www.wnba.com/comets

Indiana Fever
125 S. Pennsylvania Street
Indianapolis, IN 46204
317-917-2500
www.wnba.com/fever

Los Angeles Sparks
2151 E. Grand Avenue, #100
El Segundo, CA 90245
310-341-1000
www.wnba.com/sparks

Minnesota Lynx
600 First Avenue North
Minneapolis, MN 55403
612-673-1600
www.wnba.com/lynx

New York Liberty
2 Pennsylvania Plaza
New York, NY 10121
212-465-6073
www.wnba.com/liberty

Phoenix Mercury
201 E. Jefferson Street
Phoenix, AZ 85004
602-514-8364
www.wnba.com/mercury

Sacramento Monarchs
One Sports Parkway
Sacramento, CA 95834
916-928-0000
www.wnba.com/monarchs

San Antonio Silver Stars
One SBC Center
San Antonio, TX 78219
210-444-5050
wwww.wnba.com/stars

Seattle Storm
351 Elliot Avenue, W. #500
Seattle, WA 98119
206-217-WNBA (9622)
www.wnba.com/storm

Washington Mystics
401 Ninth St., N.W.
Washington, DC 20004
202-266-2361
www.wnba.com/mystics

What about the Minor Leagues?

Recent years have seen the resurgence of the minor leagues of basketball, despite some lean times in the 90s. Continental Basketball Association (CBA) franchises had been closing regularly around that period, and in early 2001, the head office followed. Three years earlier, in 1998, the American Basketball League (ABL) had ended its run. However, in late 2001 the future of minor league basketball began to look a little rosier.

A vastly reduced and reorganized CBA kicked off again in the fall of 2001, and it has since gone on to secure its future. Meanwhile, a newly formed American Basketball Association (ABA) has grown to more than 35 teams in this millennium. Plus the NBA itself has also gotten in on the act, creating the National Basketball Development League. This League houses young players who had been drafted by a NBA team but were later waived before they could actually play a season.

Today, the shadow circuit of American basketball is moving toward a truly innovative product not dependent on superstars like Michael Jordan to keep it alive. The non-NBA scene has never been stronger!

Current Minor League Teams

Below are the lists of the minor league teams, as they were at the time of this writing.

Continental Basketball Association (CBA) teams include Albany Patroons, Yakama Sun Kings, Butte Daredevils, Oklahoma Cavalry, Minot Sky Rockets, Pittsburgh Xplosion, Atlanta Krunk, East Kentucky Miners, Rio Grande Valley Silverados, Vancouver Dragons, and the Great Fall Explorers.

American Basketball Association (ABA) teams include Anderson Champions, Atlanta Vision, Boston Blizzard, Chicago Throwbacks, Corning Bulldogs, Detroit Panthers, First State Fusion, Georgia Gwizzlies, Halifax Rainmen, Hawaii Hurricanes, Houston Takers, Jersey Express, Long Beach Breakers, Los Angeles Push, Manchester Millrats, Maywood Buzz, Minnesota Ripknees, Monterrey Veneno, Montreal Royal, Orange County Gladiators, Orlando Aces, Palm Beach Imperials, Peoria Kings, Quebec Kebekwa, Reno Sharpshooters, Rochester Fire, Rome GA Legions, Sacramento Heatwave, San Deigo Wildcats, San Francisco Rumble, St. Louis Stunners, Strong Island Sound, Syracuse Raging Bulls, Texas Tycoons, Vermont Frost Heaves, West Texas Whirlwinds, and Westchester Phantoms.

National Basketball Development League (D-League) teams include Albuquerque T-Birds, Anaheim Arsenal, Austin Toros, Bakersfield Jam, Colorado 14ers, Dakota Wizards, Fort Wayne Mad Ants, Idaho Stampede, Iowa Energy, LA D-Fenders, Rio Grande Valley Vipers, Sioux Falls Skyforce, Tulsa 66ers, and Utah Flash.

SlamBall (SlamBall.WarnerBros.com) teams include Bandits, Bouncers, Diablos, Mob, Raiders, Rumble, Slashers, and the Steal.

ELEVEN

NASCAR Drivers

*"Kyle Busch just crowded me into the wall there.
But no hard feelings. I'll just chalk it up to hard racing.
I talked with him after the race. Everything's settled,
we're on good terms, and I got his dad's autograph."*

—CARL EDWARDS

NASCAR wasn't always a sport in which supercharged race cars battled each other on the course and drivers competed for millions of dollars in sponsorships. In fact, in the early days of stock car racing, the cars were exactly that—stock standard, and drivers who didn't have a car to race would rent a car for the weekend and run it against the competition.

NASCAR has advanced a long way since then, and today the fame of drivers within the sport has followed suit. In fact, more people attend NASCAR events each year than any other sport in North America!

Some people get to the track early and make their way to the pits in hopes of meeting their favorite drivers. Others hang around before and after time trials with a pen and paper handy. Additional enthusiasts get in touch with drivers through their official fan clubs, which are generally run by the driver's staff.

The fans will send a letter, include a self-addressed stamped envelope, join the fan club, and wait. However, not every NASCAR driver fan-club ensures you'll receive a contact opportunity with the racer in question. For example, for a membership fee of $35 a year, the Jeff Gordon Network gives you:

- An official JGN membership card
- JGN hero card with letter from Jeff
- JGN sling bag
- JGN luggage tag
- JGN die-cut air freshener
- Coupon for online store
- Access to exclusive streaming videos and photo galleries
- The Jeff Gordon monthly magazine
- Opportunity to apply for Jeff Gordon Network events

While being a member of an official fan club sometimes can help you get in touch with a driver, it isn't a guaranteed method. What works much better is to keep an eye out for a race in your town or any pre-race driver appearances. The drivers will usually turn up for autograph-signing sessions at local branches of their sponsors (such as a Home Depot or Lowe's), as well as at souvenir trailers or after-parties.

Ultimately, NASCAR drivers are fully aware that their rise to fame comes from their connection to grassroots fans. As a result, if they can find the time to sign something for you, they usually will. Just be polite, don't gush, and don't take up more of the driver's time than you should. Oh, and have something for them to sign!

Sending Fan Mail to a NASCAR Driver

To write to your favorite NASCAR driver, the best way is to join his respective fan club.

Visit **Contact Any Celebrity** (www.ContactAnyCelebrity.com) to get the direct mailing addresses for over 296 race car drivers.

NASCAR Fan Club Addresses

Jeff Burton Fan Club
P.O. Box 1160
Halifax, VA 24558

Dale Earnhardt Fan Club
4707 E. Baseline Road
Phoenix, AZ 85040

Dale Earnhardt Jr., Fan Club
4707 E. Baseline Road
Phoenix, AZ 85040

Bill Elliot Fan Club
P.O. Box 248
Dawsonville GA 30534

Jeff Gordon National Fan Club
P.O. Box 515
Williams, AZ 86048

Dale Jarrett Fan Club
4707 E. Baseline Road
Phoenix, AZ 85040

Bobby Labonte Fan Club
4707 E. Baseline Road
Phoenix, AZ 85040

Mark Martin Fan Club
P.O. Box 68
Ash Flat, AR 72513

Kyle Petty Fan Club
135 Longfield Drive
Mooresville, NC 28115

Ricky Rudd Fan Club
P.O. Box 7586
Richmond, VA 23231

Rusty Wallace Fan Club
4707 E. Baseline Road
Phoenix, AZ 85040

Some Background on Indy Racing

Indy Racing League events usually include a "fan day" on the Thursday before the race where ticket-holders can meet their heroes, and these gathering tend to get crowded. You can often miss your chance to see your favorites if you don't get there early. However, if you're in line when the doors open, you can often not only meet the Indy drivers, but also chat with the mechanics and team managers.

To contact Indy race car drivers, use the address below in the Chapter Resource section or visit their Web site for more information.

The Champ Car World Series is another grouping of races, and they returned under a new multi-year contract to ESPN in 2007. This includes the Long Beach Grand Prix and the Vegas Grand Prix. The Champ Car address is also listed in the Recommended Resources.

chapter
TWELVE

Hockey Players

*"Hockey players have fire in their hearts
and ice in their veins."*

—AUTHOR UNKNOWN

The National Hockey League (NHL) has struggled in recent years to keep up with the ever-increasing pace of the other sports that compete for people's attention—like the NBA, the NFL, Major League Soccer, and NASCAR. That's not to say, however, that it doesn't have a host of fans that dearly want to say hello to their favorite players once in a while. Hockey stars tend to be a little more personable than NBA superstars or NFL linebackers, and the reason probably is that even though they are well-paid, these athletes aren't surrounded by an entourage 24 hours a day.

Fox Sports journalist Jim Day explains, "We sometimes pull teeth to get certain professional baseball players to talk. But when it comes to hockey, players take pride in the fact that someone actually wants their autograph. It's a pride thing, and that is the big word I can use when describing a hockey player—pride. Pride in playing the game the right way, pride in being a solid individual off the ice, and pride in the fact that they feel lucky to be paid for everything in a game they love."

If you're patient, you can get an autograph from just about any NHL player as he's going in or out of the stadium or arena. On the other hand, you certainly won't get one by lobbing an index card and Sharpie pen over the glass during a game. Still, if you don't mind standing around for a few hours in the right spot outside the stadium, you'll usually have little or no problem finding your favorite player in a generous mood (especially after a win).

As with anyone else, if you're meeting a star player in person, be respectful and courteous. They'll expect you to ask them to sign something, or to even shake hands. But if you want to get them to pose for a photo with you and then wait around for two minutes while it develops so they can sign it as well, you might end up watching the player walk away.

Hockey players know they'll meet their fans on the way in (usually two or three hours before game time) and out of the stadium (half an hour after the game). But if you hang out in their hotel lobby, you may not like the response. Most players won't sign in the hotel because it's considered "their" place where they can sit back and relax. The staff in hotels usually won't allow you to hang around anyway, although you're usually welcome to stand outside on the sidewalk and hope. Restaurants are another place where players tend not to want to be bothered; however if you spot a player at the hotel bar or at a local nightclub where the team hangs out, you may just want to take a shot—or at least buy him one!

The most successful autograph collectors don't see a meeting with a star as a one-off chance to grab a signature. In fact, when a player has seen you around three or four times and you've treated him with respect and warmth, chances are he'll stop and talk once in a while. The key here is to not gush all over the players, but instead show them a level of respect.

In doing this, you demonstrate to the players that you're not a drooling fan, and that you respect them as adults and as competitors (even if they're not your only favorite team). On the other hand, if they don't have time to sign, and you say something stupid like "Yeah, well, I hear McDonalds is hiring," then you're making absolutely certain you'll never get anything out of that player—or any other player he might talk to as he passes you by.

Each stadium or arena has a place where the home and away teams come in each day and park their cars, buses, and limos. When they're coming to the stadium, chances are the security guards will keep you away. Yet when the game is over, the guards will usually back off to allow the fans a little face time. Additionally, most teams will have an early day skate around on the ice before the game, generally sometime between 10:00 A.M. and noon. At these times, the crowds are nowhere to be seen, so you can get a little space to bond with the players and shoot the breeze.

Be aware that many teams have their pre-game skates and training sessions at other smaller arenas, which can be excellent places to find celebrity contact opportunities. Despite this, you don't want to start yelling at a player across the parking lot or you'll soon find yourself surrounded by other people vying for his attention as well. Stay calm and be casual and friendly to get that signature you've been waiting for.

Be Prepared—What to Have on Hand for Signing

If you only want to meet the players, then that's all you need to do. Alternately, if you want a signature as well, then you may have to do a little strategic planning. Remember—if you don't have something for the player to sign, you're not going to get anything signed at all. So before you hit your local arena, stock up on some hockey cards. In a perfect world, it would be great to get a rookie card for everyone on the team, but that can be a serious investment of money and time.

Instead, pick a couple of your absolute favorite players and get their rookie cards. The rest of the team will have to make do with signing current cards, photos, magazine articles, jerseys, sticks, hats or pucks. Remember, if your intention is to sell these signatures, you want to give the player more than just a scrap of paper—make the signature special by having it signed on something special.

A well-known player's signature on the back of a torn ticket is great, but a signature on a team jersey becomes a genuine piece of memorabilia. If you can convince the player to get his picture taken while holding the jersey, you've just made yourself a certificate of authenticity that's actually worth something in itself. A good fallback option for autographs is the team program, since it will have pictures of all the players and can be used to gather signatures from the entire team over time.

Sending Fan Mail to an NHL Player

If you don't have the time or enthusiasm to stake out the stadium, try sending a self-addressed stamped envelope (SASE) to the player via the team. Make sure to include an index card, photo, or hockey card for the player to sign, and always be willing to lose any item if they don't send it back to you.

Most hockey teams (both NHL and minor league) will be all too happy to pass your autograph requests on to their players and coaches. In fact, it's an important part of their marketing strategies for the players to connect with their fans (you!).

Some Web sites even offer a way to write the player for an autograph. The Colorado Avalanche Web site states, "Autograph requests should be addressed to the player/coach in question, and should include a self-addressed stamped envelope (unsealed) so the player/coach can return the item to you. Do not send an item to more than one player in the same envelope. Some players receive an extremely large amount of fan mail and it may take a long period of time for a response. Fans should remember that players/coaches are not obligated to sign or return anything mailed to them. Any items are sent at your own risk; the Colorado Avalanche and its players/employees cannot and will not be responsible for any item nor guarantee its safe return."

Here's how I would break down the general rules: (1) only include one autograph request per package that you send, (2) don't send things that are valuable or heavy, (3) understand that not every player can find the time to send something back to you, and (4) always remember to include your self-addressed stamped envelope!

Remember that hockey players—like most professional athletes—usually live in different cities than the ones they represent. So if a player doesn't get back to you with a signed picture, the reason may be that it's the off-season and he's enjoying being back home. Or maybe he's climbing a mountain in the Himalayas. Or he's been traded. Or perhaps he's just lazy. But whatever the reason, it's not the hockey club's fault.

Visit **Contact Any Celebrity** (www.ContactAnyCelebrity.com) to get the best mailing addresses for over 1,013 professional hockey players.

Professional Hockey Teams

Anaheim Mighty Ducks
2695 E. Katella Avenue
Anaheim, CA 92806
1-877-WILDWING (9464)
714-704-2700
www.MightyDucks.com

Atlanta Thrashers
Centennial Tower
101 Marietta Street N.W., #1900
Atlanta, GA 30303
404-878-3300
www.AtlantaThrashers.com

Boston Bruins
One TD Banknorth Garden
Boston, MA 02114
617-624-1900
www.BostonBruins.com

Buffalo Sabres
HSBC Arena
One Seymour H. Knox III Plaza
Buffalo, NY 14203
716-855-4100
www.Sabres.com

Calgary Flames
Pengrowth Saddledome
555 Saddledome Rise SE
Calgary, AB T2P 3B9
CANADA
403-777-2177
www.CalgaryFlames.com

Carolina Hurricanes
RBC Center
1400 Edwards Mill Road
Raleigh, NC 27607
919-467-7825
www.CarolinaHurricanes.com

Chicago Blackhawks
United Center
1901 W. Madison Street
Chicago, IL 60612
312-455-7000
www.ChicagoBlackHawks.com

Colorado Avalanche
Pepsi Center
1000 Chopper Circle
Denver, CO 80204
303-405-1100
www.ColoradoAvalanche.com

Columbus Blue Jackers
Nationwide Arena
200 W. Nationwide Boulevard
Suite Level
Columbus, OH 43215
614-246-4625
www.BlueJackets.com

Dallas Stars
2601 Avenue of the Stars
Frisco, TX 75034
214-387-5500
www.DallasStars.com

Detroit Red Wings
Joe Louis Arena
600 Civic Center Drive
Detroit, MI 4822
313-983-606
www.DetroitRedWings.com

Edmonton Oilers
11230 110th Street
Edmonton, AB T5G 3H7
CANADA
780-414-4000
www.EdmontonOilers.com

Florida Panthers
One Panther Parkway
Sunrise, FL 33323
954-835-7000
www.FLPanthers.com

Los Angeles Kings
1111 S. Figueroa Street
Los Angeles, CA 90015
213-742-7100
www.LAKings.com

Minnesota Wild
317 Washington Street
St. Paul, MN 55102
651-602-6000
www.Wild.com

Montreal Canadiens
1275 St. Antoine Street West
Montreal, QC H3C 5L2
CANADA
514-932-2582
www.canadiens.com

Nashville Predators
501 Broadway
Nashville, TN 37203
615-770-PUCK (7825)
www.NashvillePredators.com

New Jersey Devils
Continental Airlines Arena
50 Route 120 North
E. Rutherford, NJ 07073
201-935-6050
www.NewJerseyDevils.com

New York Islanders
1535 Old Country Road
Plainview, NY 11803
516-501-6700
www.NewYorkIslanders.com

New York Rangers
2 Pennsylvania Plaza
New York, NY 10121
212-465-6000
www.newyorkrangers.com

Ottawa Senators
Corel Centre
1000 Palladium Drive
Kanata, ON K2V 1A5
CANADA
613-599-0250
www.ottawasenators.com

Philadelphia Flyers
3601 S. Broad Street
Philadelphia, PA 19148
215-465-4500
www.PhiladelphiaFlyers.com

Phoenix Coyotes
5800 W. Glenn Drive, #350
Glendale, AZ 85301
23-463-8800
www.PhoenixCoyotes.com

Pittsburgh Penguins
Civic Arena, Gate 9
Pittsburgh, PA 15219
602-379-2800
www.PittsburghPenguins.com

San Jose Sharks
525 W. Santa Clara Street
San Jose, CA 95113
408-287-7070
www.SJSharks.com

St. Louis Blues
Savvis Center
1401 Clark Avenue
St. Louis, MO 63102
314-622-2500
www.StLouisBlues.com

Tampa Bay Lightning
St. Pete Times Forum
401 Channelside Drive
Tampa, FL 33602
813-301-6600
www.TampaBayLightning.com

Toronto Maple Leafs
Air Canada Centre
40 Bay Street, #300
Toronto, ON M5J 2X2

Vancouver Canucks
800 Griffiths Way
Vancouver, BC V6B 6G1
CANADA
604-899-7400
www.Canucks.com

Washington Capitals
Market Square North
401 Ninth Street N.W., #750
Washington, DC 20004
202-266-2200
www.WashingtonCaps.com

Don't Forget the Minor League Teams

Remember that every great hockey superstar was once a rookie practicing his trade in Moose Jaw or Bismarck or Wichita Falls. Minor League hockey is a great place to meet tomorrow's stars today, just as in the baseball and basketball worlds. There are several leagues that serve as feeders to the NHL, most of which feature cities where the local team will sell tickets for as little as five dollars a head.

Minor League Hockey Teams

American Hockey League (AHL)
One Monarch Place
Springfield, MA 01144
473-781-2030
www.TheAHL.com

Central Hockey League (CHL)
4909 E. McDowell, #104
Phoenix, AZ 85008
800-949-8600
www.CentralHockeyLeague.com

East Coast Hockey League (ECHL)
116 Village Boulevard, #304
Princeton, NJ 08540
609-452-0770
www.ECHL.com

International Hockey League (IHL)
www.IHL-Hockey.com

North American Hockey League (NAHL)
2601 Avenue of the Stars, #400
Frisco, TX 75034
214-387-5650
www.NAHL.com

**Southern Professional Hockey League
  (SPHL)**
700 Monroe Street
Huntsville, AL 35801
828-252-7701
www.TheSPHL.com

Canadian Hockey League (CHL)
305 Milner Avenue, #201
Scarborough, ON M1B 3V4
CANADA 416-332-9711
www.CHL.ca

United States Hockey League (USHL)
Executive Corners
300 N. 5th Street, #2
Grand Forks, ND 58203
701-775-7334
www.USHL.com

chapter
THIRTEEN

Golf Pros

"We are in the entertaining business.
They want to get autographs; they want to take
something home. Whether it's a signed hat or,
you know, a program or whatever it might be."

—BERNHARD LANGER

Contacting professional golfers and getting their autographs can be tough. So much money is made from golfing memorabilia that the players have, to a large degree, shut down their autograph-signing habits. This isn't to say you can't get a golfer's autograph, but that you may either need to find the golfer shopping for groceries, or resort to buying his or her signature from a reputable dealer. If you want to go that last route, check out **Pro Tour Memorabilia** (www.ProTourMem.com). Pro Tour's autographed memorabilia is officially licensed by the PGA Tour and the Senior PGA Tour.

You can still meet your favorite golfer in a number of ways. For starters, simply go to your local golf course and say "hi" to the club professional. More often than not, the club pro has played a little golf and will know a few other pros. If he or she feels the urge, you might just be told how to get in touch with their contacts. If not, the more important task when dealing with your club pro will be to find out when the next big tournament or Pro-Am will happen.

Large golf tournaments can only exist if there are a lot of sponsors, and since every big-name player is paid a hefty appearance fee for just showing up, the expectation is that the player will do a little PR for the tournament. That's your chance to show up as well, make a little small talk, and say, "Hey, I wondered if you wouldn't mind maybe signing my program for me." The golfer may say no, but chances are he or she will be happy to sign.

In fact, most tournaments include several parties and banquets before and after the festivities. So if you can get invited, you'll most likely find a lot of players happy to talk with you. A rain delay is another great time to locate your heroes, since they can't change clothes or shower in case the rain breaks, and they'll have very little to do other than sign while they wait for the weather to get better.

Some golf stars are definitely more accessible than the others. Leading player Phil "Lefty" Mickelson has commented on his generally open attitude towards autographs and golf fans. "I understand it's the people in the gallery who come out and support the game of golf that allow myself and other players to play golf for a living," he said. "So I try to take the time and show that I respect them, whether it's to sign autographs or just acknowledge they're there."

The Pro-Am is a great way to meet your favorite golfer, but it will cost you money—and lots of it. Spaces in celebrity Pro-Ams are normally auctioned off to people with money to blow. However, if you can afford to get in the line-up, you'll not only meet your favorite golfers, but also get to play a round with them. That's got to be worth more than a signed photo in the mail, don't you think?

Thinking fast is always an important part of meeting a celebrity, and particularly regarding how to make the encounter a positive experience for everyone. In 2003, when actor Bill Murray hit a golf ball into the crowd during a Pro-Am tournament in Pebble Beach, the quick-thinking woman he'd hit came out of the gallery and asked him to sign the ball. In a situation like that, how could he not? In fact, Murray goofed around with the woman for a few minutes before he signed the ball for her and moved on.

One thing to remember if you do spot a celebrity golfer is to not rush up and be a pain on the course. Remember . . . golf may be just a simple pleasure for you. However, for the players, it's their livelihood. If you interrupt them while they're preparing for a tournament, you might end up with your head bitten off rather than getting a signed picture.

Golf fans are expected to be calm, good-natured, gentlemanly and lady-like at all times, and when they are, the pros tend to chum around with them. Unruly fans get short shrift, says Davis Love III, pointing out the difference between private and public course fans. "[Public course players] like to talk a lot. They might get mad if they are the 527th person in line and didn't get their autograph," says Love, adding that the "people who behave" get more of his time than those who get snippy.

In fact, according to Jim Furyk, being a nice person can have advantages far beyond just a signature. He actually met his wife while signing autographs on a golf course. "I was playing a practice round on Wednesday, and when I got off the golf course, there were a bunch of kids behind the green. I was signing autographs and playing with the kids and I happened to see her standing there. I said 'hi' to her, thinking she was very attractive. A friend of hers was there and he kind of introduced us, and then invited me to go to dinner with himself and his fiancé." Five years later, Furyk and the women were married.

Finally, handy items to keep with you for signing by a golf pro may include a scorecard, a tournament program, a cap, club-covers, and even a ball. But remember, without a good pen, they won't be signing anything.

Sending Fan Mail to a Golf Pro

One of the best ways to write your favorite golf pro is to send your letter to one of the associations listed below in the Recommended Resources.

In addition, almost every professional golfer is sponsored by a company— generally one that has something to do with golf wear, club manufacturing, etc. These sponsoring companies, as part of their deals, require the golfer to do PR. So if you don't have luck writing to the pro through one of the other contacts, try sending your note to the company that sponsors him or her. It's a long shot, but worth the price of a stamp for sure.

Visit **Contact Any Celebrity** (www.ContactAnyCelebrity.com) to get the direct mailing addresses of over 723 professional golfers.

chapter

FOURTEEN

Wrestlers

*"I just want my fans to know that when
I fight, you know, I'm fighting for them
. . . They're gonna love me."*

—QUINTON "RAMPAGE" JACKSON

Professional wrestling is one of the largest sectors of the entertainment industry today, having successfully moved from its former low-rent status as performance art to now earning billions of dollars a year. It has spawned computer games, music, and books, as well as huge ratings.

Although World Wrestling Entertainment (WWE) is by far the largest association in the industry, the smaller wrestling associations can be far more accessible to fans. For example, there's Ultimate Pro Wrestling (UPW), which serves as a sort of minor league feeder system to the WWE (meaning many of UPW stars go on to become big names down the road). Shows in the smaller association are more intimate, sometimes drawing no more than a few hundred fans.

Sending Fan Mail to Wrestlers

You can reach your favorite wrestler (in most cases) at his respective association by either writing to the correct address below, or visiting the association's Web site. See Recommended Resources.

Visit **Contact Any Celebrity** (www.ContactAnyCelebrity.com) to get the direct mailing addresses of over 94 professional wrestlers.

Professional Wrestling Organizations

All Pro Wrestling (APW)
21063 Cabot Boulevard, #1
Hayward, CA 94545
510-785-8396
www.AllProWrestling.com

World Wrestling Entertainment (WWE)
1241 E. Main Street
Stamford, CT 06902
203-352-8600
www.WWE.com

Ultimate Pro Wrestling (UPW)
63 Via Pico Plaza, #139
San Clemente, CA 92672
949-475-7663
www.UPW.com

FIFTEEN

Political Figures & Heads of State

.

"Meeting Franklin Roosevelt was like opening your first bottle of champagne, knowing him was like drinking it."

—WINSTON CHURCHILL

This is a short chapter, because the best way to contact politicians and heads of state is to find their office address in one of the Marquis Who's Who directories, or on their official Web site (see the chapter titled "Doing Your Research").

But here's the address you'll probably most want to keep handy:

The White House
1600 Pennsylvania Avenue N.W.
Washington, DC 20500
202-456-1111(Comments)
202-456-2461 (Fax)
comments@whitehouse.gov

Visit Contact Any Celebrity (www.ContactAnyCelebrity.com) to get the direct mailing addresses of over 149 political figures and heads of state.

chapter

SIXTEEN

Authors & Writers

"I used to save all my rejection slips because I told myself, one day I'm going to autograph these and auction them. And then I lost the box."

—JAMES LEE BURKE

Most authors do book tours when they have a new book coming out, and they make stops around the country to meet their fans and autograph copies—after you've purchased the book, of course. You can track their route to note when they might be nearby by visiting their publisher's Web site or finding a Web site for the author or their book on the Internet. Also, watch the monthly newsletters at your local Border's or Barnes & Noble.

There is also an annual book trade show, **Book Expo America (BEA)** (www.BookExpoAmerica.com), where many famous authors appear and sign books. However, a better option for the general public can be book fairs such as the *Los Angeles Times* Festival of Books (www.latimes.com/extras/festivalofbooks), where authors appear on free panels and also do book-signings at booths. Last year at this L.A. book festival, over 400 authors appeared and 97 author panels were offered.

Sending Fan Mail to Authors

One of the best ways to contact authors is through their publishing company. You may also be able to write to particular authors by email through their own Web site or a site for their book.

Visit **Contact Any Celebrity** (www.ContactAnyCelebrity.com) to get the direct mailing addresses of over 2,256 authors and writers.

Major Publishing Companies

Alyson Publications
P.O. Box 4371
Los Angeles, CA 90078
1-800-5-ALYSON
www.Alyson.com

Avon Books
HarperCollins
1350 Avenue of the Americas
New York, NY 10019
212-261-6500
www.AvonBooks.om

Bantam/Dell
Random House
1745 Broadway, Floor 3
New York, NY 10019
1-800-733-1000
www.RandomHouse.com/bantamdell

Crown Publishing
Random House
1745 Broadway, Floor 3
New York, NY 10019
1-800-733-3000
www.RandomHouse.com/crown

Doubleday
Random House
1745 Broadway, Floor 3
New York, NY 10019
1-800-733-3000
www.RandomHouse.com/doubleday

Farrar, Straus & Giroux
19 Union Square West
New York, NY 10003
212-741-6900
www.fsgbooks.com

Harcourt Inc.
6277 Sea Harbor Drive
Orlando, FL 32887
407-345-2000
www.Harcourt.com

Harper Collins
1350 Avenue of the Americas
New York, NY 10019
212-261-6500
www.HarperCollins.com

Henry Holt
175 Fifth Avenue
New York, NY 10010
646-307-5095
www.HenryHolt.com

Houghton Mifflin
222 Berkeley Street
Boston, MA 02116
617-351-5000
www.HMCO.com

Hyperion Books
77 West 66th Street, Floor 11
New York, NY 10023
www.HyperionBooks.com

Little, Brown and Company
1271 Avenue of the Americas
New York, NY 10020
www.TWBookmark.com

McGraw Hill Companies
P.O. Box 182604
Columbus, OH 43272
1-877-833-5524
www.McGraw-Hill.com

MacMillan
1400 Miller Parkway
McHenry, IL 60050
815-363-3582
www.MCP.com

Mysterious Press
Warner Books
271 Avenue of the Americas
New York, NY 10020
www.TWBookmark.com/mystery

New American Library
375 Hudson Street
New York, NY 10014
212-366-2000
www.NALAuthors.com

Oxford University Press (NY)
198 Madison Avenue
New York, NY 10016
212-726-6000
1-800-445-9714
www.OUP.com

Oxford University Press (UK)
Great Clarendon Street
Oxford OX2 6DP
UNITED KINGDOM
011-44-18-6555-6767
www.OUP.com

Penguin Putnam
375 Hudson Street
New York, NY 10014
212-366-2000
www.PenguinPutnam.com

Prentice-Hall
One Lake Street
Upper Saddle River, NJ 07458
201-236-3290
vig.PrenHall.com

Random House
1745 Broadway, Floor 3
New York, NY 10019
1-800-733-3000
www.RandomHouse.com

Scholastic Press
557 Broadway
New York, NY 10012
212-343-6726
www.Scholastic.com

Simon & Schuster
1230 Avenue of the Americas, Floor 11
New York, NY 10020
212-698-7547
www.SimonSays.com

St. Martin's Press
175 Fifth Avenue
New York, NY 10010
212-674-5151
www.StMartins.com

Time Warner Books
1271 Avenue of the Americas
New York, NY 10020
www.TWBookmark.com

chapter

SEVENTEEN

Comic Book Artists & Writers

"People still think of me as a cartoonist, but the only thing I lift a pen or pencil for these days is to sign a contract, a check, or an autograph."

—WALT DISNEY

Although most comic book creators, artists, and writers tell you where to send fan mail inside their publications, the comic book industry also takes great pains to make itself available to their fan base through conventions, expos, and fan events.

The general rule of thumb is if you wait a while, a comic convention (or "comic-con") is likely to be announced in your area, and the organizers will make all sorts of promises as to who will be there—and then most of them won't show up. Buy your ticket anyway, and take a few hundred bucks and a good Sharpie pen—because even if the people who show up aren't the people promised, they'll most likely be worth meeting.

Most comic conventions today go far beyond only comic books. They often feature actors, directors, television stars, set designers, comic artists, writers, and an assortment of retro names that will have you scratching your head trying to remember who they were. The show will usually charge around $25 for a ticket, but the attractions will last all day long, from rare film screenings to autograph sessions to bootleg comics for sale. Most conventions travel around the country so fans don't have to spend any money to travel.

What should you bring to get signed? Nothing really, unless you know someone is going to be there and you have some great piece of memorabilia sitting around relevant to that person. Usually there are plenty of items for sale at comic conventions, and you can purchase something you like to have it signed.

Prices at convention's vendor booths are usually not cheap. Still, you can pick up some really neat pieces of pop culture memorabilia if you look hard enough, and the chance to get that item signed by its creator can be something really special. This includes items like photos, posters, movie and television scripts, costumes, etc.

Comic book conventions and the comics themselves are part of a huge industry that gets bigger every year. Therefore, comic-cons are a great place to spot up-and-coming stars before their signatures become worth thousands of dollars when they really hit it big.

How do you find a comic convention in your area? It's pretty easy—just go here:

Comic Book Conventions

www.ComicBookConventions.com

The ComicBookConventions.com Web site lists all upcoming comic-cons, usually four or five per weekend, and it also announces changes to programming, cancellations, and contact information.

The better conventions come back the same time every year, such as **Comic-Con International (CCI)** (www.Comic-Con.org) and **Dragon*Con** (www.DragonCon.org). In 2007, over 100,000 fans converged at the Comic-Con International show in San Diego. It also brought out stars like Rosario Dawson, Richard Hatch, and Marc Singer.

Every corner of the country has some sort of gathering. However, even if you have to get in the car and drive a few hours to get to a good-size convention, the money spent in doing so can be gained back when you take that authentic John Byrne sketch and put it up for auction on eBay.

Visit **Contact Any Celebrity** (www.ContactAnyCelebrity.com) to get the direct mailing addresses for over 30 comic book artists and writers.

The Major Comic Conventions

The big names of the comic convention business include the following:

Comic-Con International (CCI)
P.O. Box 128458
San Diego, CA 92112-8458
619-491-2475 (Phone)
www.Comic-Con.org

The biggest and the best, Comic-Con International has become the #1 comic show in the business. Tens of thousands of enthusiasts gather every year in "America's Finest City," some flying in from across the country to listen to panels of experts, get autographs, buy memorabilia, watch special screenings of movies, and just hang out.

Dragon*Con (D*C)
P.O. Box 16459
Atlanta, GA 30321-0459
770-909-0115 (Phone)
www.DragonCon.org

A solid second in popularity and reputation, Dragon*Con takes on more of a fantasy tilt—but it's not just for Dungeons and Dragons fanatics. D*C gets bigger every year, and as the collectors grow from obsessed teenagers to well-funded adult fans, the money going through the registers keeps increasing as well.

Big Apple Comic Convention (BACC)
704 76th Street
North Bergen, NJ 07049
201-861-1414
www.BigAppleCon.com

This one is held in New York City, so of course it's big. If you live in the northeast, the Big Apple Con is the one for you.

Mid-Ohio-Con (MOC)
P.O. Box 3831
Mansfield, OH 44907
419-526-1427
www.MidOhioCon.com

The Midwest really knows how to put on a show, and M-O-C always has an interesting lineup of names. It's not the biggest comic-con around, but it has a reputation as one of the best.

Mega-Con (MC)
P.O. Box 1097
Safety Harbor, FL 34695
727-796-5725
www.MegaConvention.com

chapter

EIGHTEEN

Supermodels

*"The people who ask me for my autograph
are the people who've put me here today,
and you can't afford to forget that."*

—KATIE PRICE

Meeting in Person

The best way to meet your favorite supermodel is to attend Fashion Week, sometimes referred to as Mercedes-Benz Fashion Week or Olympus Fashion week (this depends on who the sponsor is). Although hard to get into unless you're a member of the industry, tickets can be had if you know someone in fashion or can find some for sale (check eBay). Fashion Week is held annually in the fashion capitals of the world, including New York City, Paris, London and Milan.

Fashion Week New York is the most well-known, held at Bryant Park in New York City each year. Lately the event has become even more well-known among the public, as contestants on reality shows like *Project Runway* and *The Fashionista Diaries* compete to show their winning designs at the event. Fashion Week is attended by major fashion designers, stylists, magazine editors and, of course, supermodels (who are often not only in the show, but sitting front row along with major stars as well).

You can also hit the clubs in South Beach, Miami during "Model Season," which is January through April. Because it's too cold in New York and Los Angeles for fashion shoots, the models go to where the sun is shining in Miami, and many photo shoots for upcoming spring and summer catalogs are scheduled for this time. To find out which clubs are currently the "hot spots," check Miami's monthly fashion and style magazine, *Ocean Drive*. You can usually find it at Borders and Barnes & Noble, or stop online at www.OceanDrive.com.

Sending Fan Mail to a Supermodel

To write to your favorite supermodel, you can send your letter to his or her respective agency:

Boss
www.BossModels.com

Elite
www.EliteModel.com

Ford
www.FordModels.com

Wilhelmina
www.Wilhelmina.com

To find out which agency represents which models, visit their respective Web sites.

Visit **Contact Any Celebrity** (www.ContactAnyCelebrity.com) to get the best mailing addresses for over 412 models and supermodels.

NINETEEN

Playboy Playmates

*"It's incredible to experience a different life. I was
in a very small bubble where I came from."*

—SARA JEAN UNDERWOOD

Commenting on how her life changed
after being named the 2007 Playmate of the Year

Caution: *Some links in this section contain adult content. Parental discretion
is advised.*

They're beautiful, they're sexy, and they're timeless. Playboy Playmates are more than just good-looking—they're a piece of history. That's why a signed photo of a 1967 centerfold model is worth more every month you hold onto it. Tracking down a Playmate, however, can be tough, since many of the earlier models have moved on to bigger and better things since they "did it for the art."

Sending Fan Mail to a Playmate

Thankfully, Playboy is a company that understands the value of their history. Therefore, their Web site (www.PartyWithTheBunnies.com) gives those who want to get in touch with a specific model the means to do so—albeit for a price.

Another option for contacting a Playmate is to simply write Playboy at the following address for info on where you can find one of their models:

[Playmate Name]
c/o Playboy Promotions
Playboy Enterprises International, Inc.
9242 Beverly Boulevard
Beverly Hills, CA 90210

This is a hit or miss option. There's no guarantee that what you send will be passed on to your desired Playmate. In fact, Playboy usually refuses to forward correspondence, so you need to either get lucky or plead a strong case. Even if you do get your letter through, there's no guarantee that the model will send you an autograph despite your having written her a wonderful letter and sending along a picture. Maybe she's bored. But hey, the chance of a response is worth the price of a stamp!

Visit **Contact Any Celebrity** (www.ContactAnyCelebrity.com) to get the direct mailing addresses for over 412 models and Playboy Playmates.

Many Playboy Playmates also have their own personal Web sites where they'll gladly receive your correspondence (usually by email). Some will sign something for you (for a price), others want you to buy their book first, and some want you to pay a membership free to join their site.

For information on which Playmates appeared in which issue, check the Playboy Cyber Club, which has archives of every Playmate ever:

Playboy Enterprises
www.PartyWithTheBunnies.com

Meeting in Person

One option for meeting Playmates is the Playboy Golf Scramble, which takes place every summer in cities all over the United States and Canada. These events bring in a pack of Playmates, and you can sign up to play golf with them for $400.

Playboy Golf Scramble
www.PlayboyGolf.com

Another type of Playboy happening—the "meet and greet" cigar event—is held year-round, and for these, various models (both current Playmates and Playmates from previous decades) show up. The entire purpose of these events is for the playmates to chat with you. You can find more info on these cigar events—including a complete schedule—on the www.PlayboyGolf.com Web site.

Playboy Mansion Parties

In addition to the above events, there are two types of parties actually at the Playboy Mansion: (1) the Rented Event and (2) the Hugh Hefner event.

1. The Rented Event

The Rented Event is when a company or private party rents out the Mansion. It still comes stocked with Playmates, and there can be a high ratio of women to men. This type of party happens frequently and is a sure-fire way of getting into the Mansion.

Every year, Internet marketing consultant **"The Rich Jerk"** rents out the Playboy Mansion for a networking event. Anyone can get in, as long as you buy a ticket (usually about $1,000). But what's really cool about this event is that it's not just a party; it's designed to help you network and learn how to make a lot of money as well—which means you can probably write it off as a business expense.

To find out more about The Rich Jerk and to get on his email list for an automatic invite to the next Playboy Mansion Party, visit www.PartyWithRichJerk.com.

2. Hugh Hefner Events

These parties are run by the man himself—like the Midsummer Night's Dream Party and the Playmate of the Year Party—and they're much harder to get into. Both of the parties I mentioned take place in the summer, with the Playmate of the Year Party kicking everything off in May. The largest amount of Playmates attend the Playmate of the Year Party.

According to Hollywood publicist **Rob Tencer** (www.RobTencerPR.com), if you call the Mansion to try and be put on the guest list, you'll be told the following rules (they apply to women only, as men get an automatic no). Sometimes women are allowed to bring a male guest, but they must be a celebrity. Otherwise a girl can only bring another girl.

They'll also tell you to send your bio and a photo along with your contact information to:

Playboy
10236 Charing Cross Road
Los Angeles, CA 90024

If you're approved, someone from the Mansion will call or send you an invitation. Read it, and follow the instructions. If you don't dress appropriately, you will not be allowed in. So if it's a pajama party, wear pajamas!

If you're A-list, you'll be allowed to drive onto the Mansion's property. If you're not, you'll go to the assigned parking lot and take a shuttle to the Mansion.

Good luck!

chapter TWENTY

Adult Film Stars

"I know that fame is fleeting.
I am honored that people think that way . . .
I try not to think about it in those terms."

—MARILYN CHAMBERS

Commenting on "being popular"

Caution: *The links in this section contain adult content. Parental discretion is advised.*

If you're interested in meeting your favorite porn or adult film star, you'll need to make your way west. Most events where porn stars play take place in Los Angeles or Las Vegas. To find out about adult industry parties, check the following Web sites:

Adult Video News (AVN)
www.AVN.com

XBiz
www.XBIZ.com

Gay Video News (GayVN)
www.GayVN.com

The best way to meet your favorite adult stars is to attend the **Adult Entertainment Expo** (www.AdultEntertainmentExpo.com) in Las Vegas. Held every year at the beginning of January, the Adult Entertainment Expo (home to the infamous AVN Awards) brings almost every porn star in the world to its exhibition floor where they sign autographs and take photos with fans. Make sure you purchase a fan ticket, because the ticket price for industry folks is quite steep—although both types of tickets get you into mostly the same show.

In today's world, where almost every company (especially adult ones) have a Web site, many adult stars also attend the Internext expos, which are held twice each year in Las Vegas and Miami. Internext is the trade show for adult Web sites, payment processors, toy companies and anything else adult that's online.

Internext Expo
www.Internext-Expo.com

AVN Adult Novelty Expo
www.adultnoveltyexpo.com

Adultcon
www.adultcon.com

Cybernet Expo Varies
www.cybernetexpo.com

Adult Online Europe
www.adultonlineeurope.com

There are a couple of other conventions to keep in mind as well, including the following:

Erotica L.A.
www.erotica-la.com

GayVN
www.gayvnawards.com

Erotika U.K.
www.erotica-uk.com

The XBiz Show
www.xbizsummerforum.com

Sending Fan Mail to Adult Stars

Sending fan mail to the "adult" celebrities, like with the Playboy models, can be tricky. Many of them do not want their addresses known for privacy and security reasons, and they switch agencies often (if they have one at all). The best way to contact the star is through his or her official Web site, which you can find by doing a search on Google as outlined in Chapter 3.

Visit **Contact Any Celebrity** (www.ContactAnyCelebrity.com) to get the best mailing addresses for over 50 adult film stars.

Recommended Resources

Associations & Guilds

Screen Actors Guild
www.SAG.org
SAG Actor's to Locate Line
323-549-6737

Authentication Services

Collectors Universe
www.Collectors.com

Is It Real
www.IsItReal.com

Authors & Writers

Book Expo America
www.BookExpoAmerica.com

Los Angeles Times Festival of Books
www.latimes.com/extras/festivalofbooks

Baseball Players

Major League Baseball
www.MLB.com

Basketball Players

American Basketball Association (ABA)
www.ABAAlive.com

Continental Basketball Association (CBA)
www.CBAHoopsOnline.com

National Basketball Association (NBA)
www.NBA.com

National Basketball Development League (D-League)
www.nba.com/nbdl

Women's National Basketball Association (WNBA)
www.WNBA.com

Celebrity Contact Information

The Celebrity Black Book
www.CelebrityBlackBook.com

Contact Any Celebrity
www.ContactAnyCelebrity.com

Celebrity Photos

Amazing Celebrity Photos
www.AmazingCelebrityPhotos.com

Clubs & Associations

Universal Autograph Collectors Club (UACC)
www.UACC.org

Comic Book Artists & Writers

Big Apple Comic Convention (BACC)
www.BigAppleCon.com

Comic Book Conventions
www.ComicBookConventions.com

Comic-Con International (CCI)
www.Comic-Con.org

Dragon*Con (D*C)
www.DragonCon.org

Mega-Con (MC)
www.MegaConvention.com

Mid-Ohio-Con (MOC)
www.MidOhioCon.com

Fan Clubs

International Fan Club Organization (IFCO)
www.IFCO.org

Football Players

National Football League
www.NFL.com

Golf Players

Golf News and Upcoming Events
www.Golf.com

The Ladies' Professional Golf Association (LPGA)
www.LPGA.com

Pro Tour Memorabilia
www.ProTourMem.com

Professional Golfers' Association of America (PGA)
www.PGA.org

World Golf Hall of Fame
www.WGV.com

Halls of Fame

Basketball Hall of Fame
wwwHoopHall.com

Hockey Hall of Fame
www.HHOF.com

National Baseball Hall of Fame and Museum
BaseballHallofFame.org

Professional Football Hall of Fame
www.ProFootballHOF.com

Hockey Players

National Hockey League
www.NHL.com

Magazines

Autograph Magazine
www.AutographMagazine.com

Broadcasting & Cable Magazine
www.BroadcastingCable.com

Poets & Writers Magazine
www.pw.org/mag/

Talkers Magazine
www.Talkers.com

NASCAR Drivers

Champ Car World Series
www.ChampCarWorldSeries.com

Indy Racing League
www.IndyRacing.com

NASCAR
www.NASCAR.com

News Groups

Google Groups
Groups.Google.com

Newsletters

The Pen & Quill
www.UACC.org

Playboy Playmates

Playboy
www.Playboy.com

Playboy CyberClub
www.PartyWithTheBunnies.com

Playboy Golf Scramble
www.PlayboyGolf.com

The Rick Jerk's Playboy Mansion Party
www.PartyWithRichJerk.com

Search Services

BetterWhois
www.BetterWhois.com

Contact Any Celebrity
www.ContactAnyCelebrity.com

Google
www.google.com

Internet Movie Database (IMDB
www.IMDB.com

Marquis Who's Who
www.MarquisWhosWho.com

Social Networks

Facebook
www.Facebook.com

Friendster
www.Friendster.com

MySpace
www.MySpace.com

Ning
www.Ning.com

Xanga
www.Xanga.com

Software

Photo Stamps
www.PhotoStamps.com

Stamps.com
www.Stamps.com

Supermodels

Fashion Week Daily
www.FashionWeekDaily.com

Fashion Week L.A.
www.FashionWeekLA.com

Mercedes-Benz Fashion Week
www.MBFashionWeek.com

Television Taping Tickets

Audience Associates
www.TVTix.com

Audiences Unlimited
www.TVTickets.com

Be On Screen
www.BeOnScreen.com

Hollywood Tickets
www.HollywoodTickets.com

New York TV Tickets
www.NYTix.com

On Camera Audiences
www.OCATV.com

Studio Audiences
www.StudioAudiences.com

TV Recordings
www.TVRecordings.com

Trade Publications

Billboard
www.Billboard.com

The Hollywood Reporter
www.HollywoodReporter.com

Show Business Weekly
www.ShowBusinessWeekly.com

Variety
www.Variety.com

Wrestling

All Pro Wrestling (APW)
www.AllProWrestling.com

Ultimate Pro Wrestling (UPW)
www.UPW.com

World Wrestling Entertainment (WWE)
www.WWE.com

BONUS ARTICLE

Knowing Who Does What

Hank Mendheim, Television Producer

When trying to contact celebrities, it's important to know what each person does for a celebrity: the agent, the manager and the publicist.

The Agent is the money guy. He gets paid to find the talent jobs, whether it be voice-over, on-camera, films, TV, commercials, etc. He gets paid when the talent gets paid. The Manager runs all aspects of the talent's career, including hiring and firing agents, lawyers, publicists, etc. Any business decision eventually goes through the manager.

The Publicist handles all PR requests: interviews, autographs, etc. In some cases, as with bigger celebrities, the publicist handles all decisions regarding PR without having to go back to the manager for approval. So depending on what you need, you may want to go to the manager versus the publicist.

Autographs—All autograph requests should go to the best mailing address listed for the celebrity in the **Contact Any Celebrity** online database (www.ContactAnyCelebrity.com). That doesn't mean that you will necessarily get an answer. Celebrities are dealing with so many media requests for interviews and publicity for projects that autograph requests fall last on the list. So if you request an autograph, don't expect it immediately. It may take a while.

Don't ever call to request an autograph. Write or email. Some celebrities don't want to deal with such mail for security reasons and will not open any envelopes that look suspicious or have a handwritten address. However, most enjoy receiving fan mail and will answer it accordingly.

Charitable Donations—If you're requesting money for your charity, send that request to the manager of the talent. That's a business decision and the manager will most likely decide whether or not the celebrity ever sees the request. If your charity or organization is not authorized to accept tax-deductible donations, don't even bother. Celebrities want to know that they are helping a legitimate organization. Also, they receive many requests for donations so if you get a "no," don't take it personally.

Check the **Celebrity Causes Database** (www.CelebCauses.com) to see which celebrities contribute to your type of cause. Also, Contact Any Celebrity is a great resource for checking if the celebrity could be a supporter of your charity.

In your cover letter to the manager, you should explain why you are contacting that particular celebrity. Saying "John Doe is my favorite singer so I think that it would be great if he made a donation" doesn't cut it. However, writing "John Doe has been a supporter of XYZ since 19XX and therefore we believe he will be interested in our organization" shows that you have done your homework. And be brief. Your letter should not exceed one page. They do not want to read a diary nor do they have the time.

Forget Snail Mail—(This is for official business only, not autograph requests.) This is the technology age. I tend to send an email first if I can track down the address and then I'll follow up with a fax. Email addresses are actually quite easy to figure out for the big PR firms, especially if you do a Google search.

Contact Any Celebrity may also have the email addresses in addition to the land address. You could also call the PR firm and get a fax number (and there is nothing wrong with calling back to make sure they got the fax). I can't tell you how many times I call the next day to touch base only to be told that they never got my fax. So fax it and then call them to let them know it's there.

Common Autograph Terms

ADS—Autograph Document, Signed: A document written in the hand of the signer. (Plural ADsS)

ALS—Autograph Letter, Signed: A letter written in the hand of the person who signed it. (Plural ALsS)

ANS—Autograph Note, Signed: A note written in the hand of the person who signed it. (Plural ANsS)

AQS—Autograph Quotation, Signed: An autographed quotation written entirely in the hand of the signer. (Plural AQsS)

Autopen—A device that uses a pen to duplicate a person's signature.

Carte-de-visite—A portrait photograph, usually full-length, mounted on a small card.

DS—Document, Signed: A document that is printed and originally signed (Plural DsS).

FDC—First Day Cover: An envelope with a postmark issued on the date and in the city a stamp is issued. Sometimes collected autographed.

IPS—Inscribed Photograph, Signed: A photo bearing an inscription or personalization by the signer. (Plural IPsS)

LS—Letter, Signed: A letter written by someone other than the signer. (Plural LsS)

SB—Signed Book

SP—Signed Photo (Sometimes shown as PS)

SASE—Self-Addressed Stamped Envelope

Secretarial—Signed by a secretary or staff member.

TD—Typed Document

TDS—Typed Document, Signed: A typed signed document (Plural TDsS)

About the Author

Jordan McAuley is the Founder and President of **Contact Any Celebrity** (www.ContactAnyCelebrity.com), a service located in West Hollywood, California. Contact Any Celebrity helps businesses, nonprofits, authors, and the media get in touch with over 54,000 celebrities worldwide. He is also the editor of the best-selling *Celebrity Black Book* (www.CelebrityBlackBook.com).

After majoring in Motion Picture Business and English Literature at the University of Miami, Jordan moved to Hollywood. In L.A., he worked at a movie production company and a large Beverly Hills talent agency as an agent's assistant. These experiences—combined with working at Wilhelmina Models in South Beach during college, plus internships at CNN and Turner Entertainment—provided him with insider knowledge on the best ways to contact celebrities.

Today **Contact Any Celebrity** is known internationally as the most accurate source of celebrity contact information due to Jordan's extensive experience and personal entertainment industry contacts. Jordan's online database contains the best contact information for over 54,000 celebrities worldwide (including mailing address, agent, manager, publicist, production company, and charitable cause) plus info for over 7,000 celebrity representatives and over 4,000 entertainment companies (phone, fax, and email addresses).

Jordan and **Contact Any Celebrity** have been featured on CNN and by such national media as *USA Today*, *Entrepreneur*, *The Village Voice*, *Us Weekly*, and *Sirius Satellite Radio*. He is also recommended in several best-selling books including Timothy Ferris's instant *New York Times* best-seller *The 4-Hour Workweek*, Dan Kennedy's *The Ultimate Marketing Plan*, Dan

Poynter's *Self-Publishing Manual,* and John Kremer's *1001 Ways to Market Your Books* (which includes a chapter by Jordan on how to get celebrity book endorsements).

For more information on Jordan and his books, products and services, visit his official Web site at www.JordanMcAuley.com.

"I stopped believing in Santa Claus when I was six. Mother took me to see him in a department store and he asked for my autograph."

—SHIRLEY TEMPLE

LaVergne, TN USA
05 February 2010
172084LV00009B/29/P